THE GROUND ZERO CROSS

BRIAN J. JORDAN, OFM

Copyright © 2017 by Brian J. Jordan, OFM.

Library of Congress Control Number:		2017906458
ISBN:	Hardcover	978-1-5434-1859-0
	Softcover	978-1-5434-1858-3
	eBook	978-1-5434-1857-6

All rights reserved. No part of this book may be reproduced or transmitted
in any form or by any means, electronic or mechanical, including photocopying,
recording, or by any information storage and retrieval system,
without permission in writing from the copyright owner.

Copyright © 2015 Catholic News Service Origins – CNS Documentary Service
Reprinted with permission of CNS.

This is a work of fiction. Names, characters, places and incidents either are the
product of the author's imagination or are used fictitiously, and any resemblance
to any actual persons, living or dead, events, or locales is entirely coincidental.

Any people depicted in stock imagery provided by Thinkstock are models,
and such images are being used for illustrative purposes only.
Certain stock imagery © Thinkstock.

Printed in the United States of America.

Rev. date: 05/20/2017

To order additional copies of this book, contact:
Xlibris
1-888-795-4274
www.Xlibris.com
Orders@Xlibris.com
761190

CONTENTS

DEDICATION

This book is to dedicated to:

THE UNION CONSTRUCTION WORKERS WHO SERVED
AT GROUND ZERO THAT WAS EIGHTY PERCENT OF THE
RECOVERY WORKFORCE
Special Remembrance of Edward. J. Malloy, past president of the New
York City Building Construction and Trades Council

NEW YORK CITY POLICE DEPARTMENT; FIRE
DEPARTMENT OF NEW YORK CITY; OFFICE OF
EMERGENCY MANAGEMENT OF NYC AND THE PORT
AUTHORITY POLICE DEPARTMENT
Special Remembrance of Richard Sheirer, a dedicated public servant
for many years

FAMILY MEMBERS OF THE VICTIMS OF 9/11 AT THE
WORLD TRADE CENTER WHO HELPED SAVE THE
GROUND ZERO CROSS
Immense Gratitude To Jane Pollicino

Acknowledgements

I would like to thank the following people who were extremely influential on the writing and publication of this book. First, my parents Gerard and Eileen Jordan—who not only cooperated with God's plan of Creation to bring me into the world—but also taught me how to pray and to fight for worthy causes.

For the friars of Holy Name Province of the Order of Friar Minor and especially for our past provincial, John Felice, O.F.M, who graciously led us through the horror and pain in the aftermath of 9/11. He was the spiritual anchor that kept our Franciscan friars together. For Kevin Tortorelli, O.F.M., who meticulously proofread this manuscript and participated in the Final Blessing of the Cross into the National 9/11 Memorial Museum on July 23, 2011.

For the well-known authors, Peter Quinn and Terry Golway. Their expertise and publication experience were generously shared and proved to be invaluable. Both Peter and Terry influenced this middle-aged Irishman to write with purpose and firm conviction.

For my colleagues at St. Francis College, Brooklyn, Professors Francis Greene and Gregory Tague. Their helpful comments were a guiding light for the development of this manuscript. Victoria Prestia, a St. Francis College graduate, edited and professionally arranged this manuscript to be in excellent shape and reader friendly.

For the friars of Immaculate Conception Province of the Order of Friars Minor especially Patrick Boyle, O.F.M., Orlando Ruiz, O.F.M., and Joaquin Mejia, O.F.M., with whom I live in fraternity in Our Lady of Peace Friary in Gowanus, Brooklyn. I am grateful to them for their unswerving fraternal support, patience with my writer's block and compassionate understanding when I had an occasional "Dark Night of the Soul." They were real brothers in Our Holy Father St. Francis of Assisi!

Finally, for all my brothers and sisters who are union construction workers in the greater New York City area! I am truly inspired by your patriotism, prayer and professionalism. I hope and pray that someday the whole world will know that you met and overcame one of the greatest challenges in contemporary history of New York City. In late September, 2001, you were given a mandate for the demolition and cleanup of Ground Zero within a certain period of time that most experts considered this impossible. Not only did you complete this mandate under budget and well before the time allotted but you did this under extremely delicate conditions without a single fatality nor serious injury during those nine months. I respectfully request that the keepers of the New York City archives include this unique legacy in present and future history books. Do not forget the amazing contribution of union construction workers at Ground Zero!

CHAPTER 1

The Cross – September 11, 2001 – February 14, 2002

"History", Stephen said, "is a nightmare where I am trying to awake from."

- James Joyce, *Ulysses*.

On the morning of September 11, 2001, the Franciscan friars of St. Francis of Assisi Parish on 135 W. 31st St. in Midtown Manhattan of which I, Brian Jordan, am a part of, began Morning Prayer at 8:10 AM in the lower church of the parish. Laypeople and friars prayed together the Liturgy of the Hours which lasted about ten minutes. Immediately after prayers, my fellow friar, Father Mychal Judge, who was seated in the same pew as I was, sprang up with his ever present smile and said to me, "Hey Brian, have a good day. See you later!" That was the last I ever saw Mychal Judge, my good friend and mentor. I first met him when I was a junior at Siena College, Loudonville, New York in early September, 1976 – twenty five years later, nearly to the day, on September, 2001, I said goodbye to him forever and did not even realize it until later that day. Mychal went to his room to take care of his head cold while I went on a hospital call up in Washington Heights, Manhattan. Like the rest of New York City, none of us expected what was about to happen within the next few hours.

After attending to a child from the Dominican Republic who received a life-saving heart surgery at New York Presbyterian Hospital through the generous assistance of Governor George Pataki, New York State Surgeon General, Dr. Antonia Novello MD first informed me that both Towers were hit by airplanes as was the Pentagon. "Three planes in three key locations is more than a coincidence", I said to myself. I then bolted through the doors and attempted to get downtown by subway. I discovered that subway service was suspended in Manhattan. Even though I was a marathoner, I was not about to run in my Franciscan habit and in sandals from 168th St. back to St. Francis of Assisi. I decided to take a cab but there were no yellow cabs to be found. I managed to share one of the livery cabs around the hospital with a young Latina mother who was also trying to get downtown (she was trying to get to her daughter who was a sophomore in a gifted West Side high school). While we were journeying down Broadway, the driver put on radio channel WINS 1010. Radio reporter John Montone graphically and dramatically described the collapse of both Towers. Tower II, the second to be hit, was the first to go down at 9:58 AM. Tower I, the first to be hit, was the second to go down at 10:28 AM. The driver, young mother and I were equally devastated by this stark revelation. How could the Towers come down so quickly? We thought they were invincible. I will never forget the words, the syntax, and the emotion in John Montone's voice that morning of September 11, 2001 (henceforth, this date will be called "9/11"). I am not sure whether I should thank him or hug him. Perhaps both? Someday, I will.

At Broadway and W.72nd St., traffic came to a halt. The traffic lights were not working and crosstown traffic was heavy. I could not wait any longer. I paid my fare and jumped out of the car. I walked south on Broadway, on the left-hand side. All I saw were dazed and confused pedestrians walking north either trying to get to their destinations or fleeing from the World Trade Center. Roughly one third were covered in dust, partially or completely. All of a sudden, a strange realization came over me. At Broadway and W. 59th St., it seemed like I was the only person walking south towards the World Trade Center. To this day, this memory remains as one of the eeriest and loneliest moments of my entire life. It was not until W. 44th St. that I met another person walking briefly southward, then a left for the Port Authority Terminal. I turned south on 7th Ave. and finally made it back to my office, the Franciscan Immigration Center, at St Francis. The whole church was filled with people frightened because they could not get home. All public transportation was suspended. My brother friars gave the people water, use of the bathroom, and a few welcoming words – no one knew what the next few hours would bring.

Around 2:15 PM I decided to walk down to St. Vincent's Hospital and see if I could be of assistance. I went to my room and put on my running shoes under my Franciscan habit. I took Holy Water and a pair of brass knuckles I received as a birthday gift from a Puerto Rican family from my first parish, Holy Cross in the Southeast Bronx, in 1984. The Holy Water was for blessing the dead and injured. The brass knuckles were a measure of insurance just in case there was a need to repel a potential terrorist ground attack. I was heading for the front door of the friary when Francis DiSpigno, O.F.M., a fellow friar, told me a preliminary report just in from a city agency indicated that Father Mychal Judge, O.F.M., Chief Chaplain of the Fire Department of New York City was killed at the World Trade Center. I was stunned and speechless! *I can't believe it. How can this be?* I thought to myself. I had a decision to make, and I had to make it right away – would I sit on my backside in the friars' refectory and cry for my loss *or* go down to the World Trade Center and minister among the people like Mychal Judge was doing? I decided to walk to the World Trade Center (subsequently now abbreviated as W.T.C.).

On the way, I dropped by St. Vincent's Hospital on 7th Ave. and W. 12th St. Outside the hospital building there were many doctors, nurses and other medical personnel patiently awaiting injured patients who would never arrive. I also noticed a large number of clergy of other faiths waiting to give counsel and consolation to the injured. One of the nurses I met through past pastoral visits to the hospital came up to me with an earnest expression. She grabbed my hand and said, in an emphatic voice, "Get the hell out of here! We are top-heavy with doctors, nurses, clergy, whoever. We don't need you. Go somewhere else where you are needed." I did not take that as a rejection but an admonition. She actually did me a favor. I went where I was needed – Ground Zero.

I then turned right towards the West Side Highway and then south to Chambers St. There in front of me I saw for the first time a glimpse of the remains amid the smoke, the incessant crying, the looks of horror and shocked expressions on many faces, including my own. I comforted and consoled a great number of people who were still searching for fathers, mothers, spouses, brothers, sisters, fiancées, girlfriends, boyfriends, close confidantes, whoever. There was no cell phone service at all. Everyone was deeply confused and unsure what was going on. I stayed there for a few hours and met a fellow priest from the Diocese of Brooklyn, Monsignor David Cassato, pastor of Saint Athanasius parish, Brooklyn and NYPD police chaplain. David and I spoke for a while and I told him that Father Mychal Judge was among the dead as were key fire department personnel among others. I noticed the Salvation Army giving water and some light blankets to the bereaved. I was comforted by their presence. We then heard an angry voice shout out, "Evil has triumphed!" I did not respond directly to that person but turned around to Monsignor Cassato and said, "No... we have seen evil at its worst, but goodness at its best!" I shook David's hand and walked to the other side of Chambers St.

While gazing at a pile of smoldering smoke and fire, a young captain from the First Precinct came up to me and noticed the Holy Water in my right hand and said, "Well Father, you are going to be busy with that soon." I told him I agreed, but I thought he meant for the injured. When I asked him quietly if I could come through the barrier and start blessing people and the site itself, he said no because he had received strict orders to let no one through. I told him I understood. I recalled how my mentor Mychal Judge, who died on that same site only hours before, loved to quote from the Gospel of Matthew where Jesus said, "I come not to be served, but to serve!" I told him that I was not here for myself, but for others. As I turned to walk away, the young captain called out in a loud voice and asked me to talk to him one-on-one. He whispered in my ear to go down to a separate entrance on Chambers St. I met him there and he assigned me to an officer in a hazmat suit. The captain said, "Father, you have your Holy Water – here are a pair of gloves and a mask to protect your face." He motioned me to the pile and said, "Go to work." I then went with the officer and started blessing not the injured, but to my horror bodies and body parts. This was the first day that I performed this task, one I would continue to do for the next nine months.

GOD'S HOUSE – September 23, 2001

On Sunday morning, September 23rd, around 10 AM, I presided at a Mass near the NYPD command center on Vesey St., a block and a half from the W.T.C. site going towards the Hudson River. There were about 25 people who were either first responders or medical and counseling unit personnel. After Mass, I walked around West St. and asked if anyone who could not attend Sunday Mass wanted to receive Holy Communion as I still had consecrated hosts. Around 11 AM, a tall, hulking figure dressed in a hard hat, blue overalls, construction boots, and bright yellow vest came up to me and asked, "Do you want to see God's House?" I thought to myself, *Either this guy just got released from Bellevue Psychiatric Hospital or he's looking for a local house of worship.* I explained to him that St. Peter's Church was about 2 blocks away. I was about to give him directions when he blurted out loudly, "No, no, I don't mean some built church from the past. I want to show you God's House in the present."

Out of curiosity I agreed to follow him, but at the same time, I purposely walked behind him just in case he had well and truly gone mad, which would be quite understandable given the conditions we were enduring from the savage attack that took place a mere 12 days before. As we approached the remains of the W.T.C. 6 building, I saw the hand-painted sign on the right-hand side of the entrance that read, in bright yellow, "GOD'S HOUSE." It was dark inside the wreckage of the building. The burly construction worker identified himself as Frank Silecchia, a laborer from Local 731 of the Laborers International Union of North America, LIUNA. He asked me to peer inside closely, and to look for an object which he refused to identify. As two FDNY firefighters entered in complete silence and reverence, I saw exactly what they saw – a "cross-like" beam on top of the debris with grey covered insulation material hanging on the left side as though it were the Shroud of Turin[1]. I was utterly overwhelmed by the sight of it. I stood there for at least 3 minutes – I was so stunned I couldn't think to speak. Once I recovered from the initial shock I marveled to Frank and the two dedicated FDNY firefighters that God was truly present among us.

I talked to Frank for about an hour and discovered that he was born half Italian Catholic and half Jewish. He is now a born again Christian. He instantly asserted that this was a sign of faith from God. I immediately concurred, and promised that I would do all I could to preserve this cross-like beam. This sign of faith should be put in the public eye so people can see that God never abandoned the world on 9/11. I made that firm promise to Frank and I have remained faithful to that promise throughout the many challenges and battles I experienced with all types of bureaucracy over the years.

FIRST DEPUTY MAYOR – JOSEPH LHOTA

In the summer of 2000, I got to know Joseph Lhota quite well as the First Deputy Mayor under then Mayor Rudy Giuliani. We had an excellent rapport even before 9/11 and he would always be the go-to guy in the Giuliani administration. I called Joe the day after I first saw the cross-like beam and asked him if the City could negotiate with all other concerned agencies about erecting said cross-like beam in public and onsite. My rationale was my firm belief (then, and even more so now) that this "Cross" would serve as a sign of comfort and consolation not only

---

1   Shroud of Turin – a burial shroud traditionally believed to be the burial shroud of Jesus Christ and kept as a venerated relic in the cathedral of Turin, Italy.

for family members and friends who lost loved ones on 9/11, but also for all those who worked on the rescue and recovery operation – uniformed personnel, construction workers, volunteers and government agencies who served on that memorable 16 acre site.

Joe agreed to my request, and immediately went into action. On September 26, 2001, I received a call from Commissioner Ken Holden of the Department of Design and Construction (DDC) of New York City who asked me when I would like to have the ceremony to erect the cross-like beam in public. I thought about it for about 20 seconds - October 4th. It had to be that day, no, it could *only* be that day. When Ken asked me why I chose October 4th, I immediately responded by stating that October 4th is "the Feast of St. Francis of Assisi, the patron saint of ecology – Ground Zero is sacred ground!" Ken agreed to that date and directed construction workers to begin preparations for the installation ceremony.

BLESSING OF THE GROUND ZERO CROSS - October 4, 2001

From what I was told by Frank Silecchia, crane operators from Local 14, 14-A and 15 of the Operating Engineers, with the permission of the company that owned the crane, extracted the cross-like beam and laid it on the ground by the corner of West St. and Vesey St. During the evening of October 3rd (in which Franciscans all over the world were celebrating the Transitus, or the passing, the death, of St. Francis of Assisi), ironworkers from Local 40 led by Willie Quinlan, steamfitters from Local 638, electricians from Local 3 and other Building Trades members gave their own time to fulfill this project. They refused to be paid for what they believed was a sacred work. Both the labor and material used to erect the cross-like beam on top of a concrete abutment were all donated. This began my ministry among union construction workers when this Cross was raised on October 4, 2001. Over 400 construction workers, uniformed personnel, government agencies and volunteers all witnessed the blessing ceremony, during which I blessed with Holy Water the four sides of the Cross with the Blessing Prayer of St. Bonaventure – the God of the North, the God of the South, the God of the East and the God of the West.

Accompanying me for this blessing of the Cross of Ground Zero was the discoverer of the Cross, Frank Silecchia together with a Port Authority officer, a NYC police officer, a FDNY firefighter, supervisor Bob Stewart of the AMEC Construction Company, and two other union construction workers. We prayed together, and while we sang "God Bless America", two crane operators from Local 14, 14-A and 15 let out a thunderous blast from their cranes at which all applauded and shouted in praise of "God Bless America". It was one of the most emotionally cathartic moments of my life. I was right – this Cross at Ground Zero has given, and will continue to provide, comfort and consolation for many family members of 9/11 victims and recovery workers at Ground Zero. Why? Many recovery workers such as firefighters, police officers, construction workers and other city, state and federal agencies witnessed the carnage at 9/11. They helped pick up bodies and collect body parts. They sought solace at the Ground Zero Cross while hoping for some type of explanation as to why this mass destruction occurred. Media Stories by Mae Cheng and Jennifer Steinauer reported that the Cross had become the centerpiece of the search for answers and healing.

One such story by Jennifer Steinauer of the New York Times had one of the best descriptions of what actually occurred in "A Nation Challenged: The Site: A Symbol of Faith Marks a City's Hallowed Ground". She states that "At the ceremony yesterday, a crowd of workers, nuns, firefighters, police officers and others watched as the priest reached the beam. It had been moved by crane to what once was the West Street walkway. A welder had attached newly minted state quarters to the foot of the Cross. Names of some of the dead and 'God Bless Our Fallen Brothers' had been etched into it. Bagpipes played 'Amazing Grace' as the bucket carrying Father Jordan, a police officer, a firefighter and others, reached the Cross. Sprinkling holy water from his aspergillum on each side of the Cross, Father Jordan prayed: 'By the grace and love of Almighty God, to the north, I bless this cross in the name of the Father, the Son and the Holy Spirit', and then repeated the blessing for east, west and south. Some watched silently. Some cried. Some just smoked cigarettes. 'Keep playing bagpipes', Father Jordan shouted. A group of workers holding hands sang 'God Bless America'. A nun prayed while trying to turn off her buzzing cellphone. 'You can never destroy the spirit of America', Father Jordan said and the crowd cheered: 'USA, USA'. Then the priest blessed rescue dogs Atlas and Keifer and their veterinarians" (To learn about other stories like this, the citations regarding Cheng may be useful).

Considering the impact this Cross has had on all those involved in 9/11, I truly must express my heartfelt thanks to my very good friend, Joe Lhota, who made sure everything would go as planned. He acted not only on behalf of Mayor Rudy Giuliani but also on behalf of all who have found and continue to find comfort and hope in that Cross.

MEMORABLE MASSES BY THE CROSS – October 7, 2001 – February 13, 2002

All the governing agencies that comprised the authority on the 16 acre site agreed that there would be only one religious service onsite and that people from other religious backgrounds were allowed to participate. I was the only religious official to be permitted to say Sunday Mass and other religious celebrations onsite. Other religious services were allowed offsite, but outside the perimeter of the W.T.C. site. By early October, Ground Zero was still considered a rescue site even though there had been no survivors since the early days after 9/11. Even so, we still prayed for hope in those Masses during early and mid-October. By November, it was clear that the site would now be a recovery site and that the demolition of buildings and the removal of debris would now be the focus. A budget was given, and a timeline was issued as well.

For these Masses, we needed an altar – Local 608 of the Carpenters Union generously crafted a makeshift altar that was built and blessed for Sunday Mass, October 14th. Since it was Hispanic Heritage Month and Columbus Day was approaching, I offered a special prayer over the altar and was joined by those present who spoke Italian and Spanish. The prayer recalled that St. Joseph was a carpenter and that Jesus himself likely learned the trade as well.

During the first few weeks of October into November, Mass attendance grew from 25 people to about 100. Although I celebrated most of the Masses by the Cross at Ground Zero, I missed some Sundays such as November 3, 2001 when I ran the New York City Marathon and celebrated a Mass for first responders near the starting line in Staten Island. Thankfully, Father Christopher Keenan, O.F.M., the new fire department chaplain and fellow friar, celebrated the weekly Sunday Masses when I could not be present, about 5 times throughout the nine month recovery period.

MIDNIGHT MASS AND CHRISTMAS DAY MASS

Recovery workers were on round the clock shifts – the recovery operation was 24/7. Workers and safety personnel were ever-present on the sacred 16 acre site. Many recovery workers wanted to have a Midnight Mass on the sacred ground, as well as a Christmas Day Mass. I gladly complied with their spiritual requests.

MIDNIGHT MASS

One hour before Midnight Mass on Monday evening, December 24, 2001, the FDNY firefighters discovered the body of a fellow firefighter. We observed the customary ritual of escorting the honored dead in a body bag draped in a NYC FDNY flag before being placed in a firefighter vehicle headed towards the mortuary. It was the coldest night of the recovery operation to date, but a stranger sort of "chill" went even further into the hearts and souls of the firefighters when they discovered one of their beloved brothers one hour before Christmas Day. These brave FDNY firefighters brought the body of their brother firefighter out in a solemn procession to the FDNY EMT ambulance.

There were about 150 persons present for this solemn Midnight Mass, mostly uniformed personnel plus construction workers. Other workers who were charged with cleaning the buildings also participated. Not all were Catholic nor did it much matter since these were war-like conditions and we were literally in the "trenches". A cold, strong wind blew up, and hosts went flying through the air. No one walked away to get warm. We all stayed and braved the elements. We all knew this was sacred ground by the Cross at Ground Zero. When I raised the chalice and prayed out aloud, "Do this in memory of me," these words had new meaning for the many present, including two Muslim cleaning workers who participated in the Mass and prayed for all who died – Christians, Jews, Hindus, Buddhists, Shintos, Taoists, atheists, agnostics and yes, even Muslims. Dean Murphy of the New York Times wrote this account of the two Masses: "Father Jordan has been saying Mass every Sunday since September at the base of a split beam found by ironworkers in the rubble of 1 World Trade Center. The beam fell in the perfect shape of a cross and immediately became an inspiration for many Christians and others working at Ground Zero. On Christmas Eve, two Muslims were among the people who attended Midnight Mass there. Father Jordan said, 'To feel moved by the Christmas services was not about being Roman Catholic, the congregants said yesterday. Many of them were not. It was more about taking the time, about half an hour or so, to stop and think and to feel the emotions of the past 15 weeks at the spot where it all happened. Even with all the funerals, tributes and memorial services since Sept. 11, many of the people closest to the devastation had not allowed themselves that half hour.'

Yes, it was strange to talk about the birth of Christ amid the suffering and mass murder at Ground Zero. However, in both homilies, I reminded all participants that the purpose of Christmas is not merely to celebrate the birth of Jesus Christ. More importantly, it is about the second coming of

Jesus Christ. As in the words of our Nicene Creed, in the second coming, "He will judge among the living and the dead." In other words, the dead will never be forgotten at Ground Zero – especially on Judgment Day.

Ironically, both the Christmas Eve Midnight Mass and Christmas Day Morning Mass were the coldest days of the entire nine month rescue period. Masses were still being offered each Sunday after Christmas at 10:30 AM. We chose 10:30 AM because it coincided with the time the second Tower went down at 10:28 AM on 9/11. The weather for all the Masses during the winter of 2001-2002 was relatively mild. The good weather was one of the primary reasons why the recovery period went smoothly and resulted in being under budget and completed well before the allotted time.

FEAST OF THE HOLY FAMILY - December 30, 2001

The Feast of the Holy Family always occurs on the Sunday immediately following Christmas. What made this particular Mass so significant was that many family members of loved ones who died on 9/11 were present. One widow named Jane Pollicino from Wantagh, Long Island, lost her husband in one of the Towers. She regularly attended Sunday Mass and brought some of her family members as well. In another significant moment then Mayor Rudy Guiliani came by for his last official Mass at Ground Zero as Mayor. Earlier in the morning, Time Magazine named him "Man of the Year" for his heroic leadership regarding the aftermath of the horrific 9/11 attack. The Mayor looked quiet and humble during the proclamation of the Gospel of John. On a later occasion, Mayor Guiliani told me that he recalled those Gospel words when he was an altar boy in his home parish in Brooklyn, N.Y.

JANUARY MASSES AND INTERNATIONAL PARTICIPANTS

During the Masses in January, the majority of participants were no longer greater New York City residents who were recovery workers, volunteers or family members of victims from the New York area. All of a sudden, a large number of European families and Latino families began to participate. Most came just for the one Mass on the Feast of the Three Kings on January 6th, the feast of the Epiphany when the Three Magi from the East came to Bethlehem to adore the newborn Jesus Christ. I acknowledged all those who traveled from afar to be present for this Mass and to stand on this sacred ground – sacred ground just like Bethlehem.

This came with a revelation. We realized we were celebrating a birth not a funeral Mass. We were praying for hope and the gift of salvation -- two gifts that are far more meaningful than gold, frankincense and myrrh.

I never asked if everyone present was Catholic. I presumed they acted in good will and I valued their presence. They lost a loved one and that was all that mattered. This was not only an American tragedy but an international one as well. From what I gathered at the NYC Medical Examiner's office, about 80 nations lost loved ones in the Towers. The United States, Great Britain, Pakistan, and Mexico appear to have lost the largest numbers of loved ones. Many Irish families and members of the local Irish consulate showed up as a sign of solidarity with the many Irish Americans who died on 9/11, particularly from the FDNY, PAPD, NYPD, Cantor Fitzgerald and union construction workers. On the one hand, for those who hailed from the greater New York City area, it was an American tragedy. For everyone else outside the country, it was an international tragedy. No matter what perspective one had, it was a personal tragedy in the classic sense. It produced mindless horror, shattering souls and breaking hearts.

ASH WEDNESDAY

Ash Wednesday arrived on February 13, 2002. Many of the recovery workers requested ashes on site. I received permission to conduct a Mass that day and, after Mass, distributed Ashes. It dawned on me while preparing the homily for that memorable Ash Wednesday Mass that the traditional words for the distribution of Ashes were, "Remember that you are dust and from dust you shall return". I felt that these words might not be appropriate at this particular service in which the clear majority were overwhelmingly uniform services – FDNY, NYPD, PAPD, the Sanitation Department, union construction workers, some volunteers, the Salvation Army and the American Red Cross. I felt a moral dilemma and asked some of the firefighters, police, and construction workers for their take on those traditional words as opposed to using the new words, "Reform your life and believe in the good news of the Gospel". The majority said that the traditional words would just escalate a feeling of a perpetual Ash Wednesday.

I did not want to say, "Remember you are dust and to dust you shall return". There was dust everywhere, whether it be from the burned buildings or human remains. They asked me to make a prudential judgment. I chose to use the new words because I believed that "reform your life" was a better way of grasping a sense of hope in these tough days, rather than being formally reminded that someday we will die and return to dust. They already knew every day they worked or volunteered on the worksite that this was sacred ground. At a Mass and at the distribution of ashes, they were already living Ash Wednesday every day. My ministerial task was to provide hope through the message of conversion which lies at the heart of Lent. It was not simply a matter of the molecular rearrangement of the body. It was about hope for the eternal soul.

TRANSFER OF THE CROSS – St. Valentine's Day, February, 14, 2002

In early January, 2002, DDC Commissioner Ken Holden called me asking to have a one-on-one meeting. He informed me that due to the good weather, the demolition and cleanup operations of West St. were ahead of schedule. Since the Cross was located on the corner of West St. and Vesey St., Ken believed that West St. needed to be opened up for a variety of reasons including traffic flow each way on West St. He then asked me for a date to transfer the Cross to another part of the site which was determined to be near the corner of Church St. and Cortland St., but still within the confines of the site. Furthermore, he wanted the transfer to be done before the third week of February 2002. He predicted that the proposed new site would probably be in use at least two years before new building took its place. I agreed to the transfer and solicited dates from a number of recovery workers and family members of victims. By consensus, we agreed that February 14th, the Feast of St. Valentine, would be the transfer date and rededication ceremony. We chose St. Valentine's Day not for the celebration of romantic love, but because the Saint was a martyr. He died for what he believed in and was a witness to his faith. That was the reason for the date of the transfer – to highlight the meaning of martyrdom!

As with the first dedication ceremony on October 4, 2001, all Building Trades union members donated their time and expertise to transfer the Cross from West St. and Vesey St. on the night of February 13, 2002 and set it atop a brand new structure within the site that was opposite the Century 21 store by the corner of Church St. and Cortland St. All building material was donated by the Bovis Lend Lease construction company and the flatbed truck that transported the Cross was donated by the Teamsters Local 282. The brief ceremony was at 10:30 AM and, again, the Cross was blessed with Holy Water. There was a much smaller crowd this time since local supervisors and foremen did not give time off for their workers. Although we abided by an economy of expression, it was still a meaningful and inspirational ceremony. In fact, one of the Local 14, 14-A Operating Engineers, Harold Rochelle, yelled out loud, "Hey, we can now have church by Church Street!" All the participants applauded and shouted their approval of that apt phrase. It clearly resonated with this worshipping community with each contributing individual still searching for some measure of closure to this terrible tragedy.

MASSES BY THE GROUND ZERO CROSS – March 2002 – June 2002

The new site proved to be a greater distance from the "Taj Mahal" (the huge, white colored tent that contained the mandatory sprinkling water for all those entering the tent as well as showers for all recovery workers). The Taj Mahal by Chambers St. and West St. was also a gathering place where recovery workers, volunteers and family members of victims gathered around to eat and drink soft beverages or coffee. The tent was supervised by the Salvation Army, of which I cannot express sufficient gratitude for all the selfless, altruistic work they consistently offered. Many participants often met on Sunday mornings in the Taj Mahal before Mass and then returned there after Mass. The Salvation Army will always have a special place in my heart especially for all the people who came from around the country to volunteer in two week shifts.

ST. PATRICK'S DAY MASS – March 17, 2002

The third Sunday of March was St. Patrick's Day. Although it was considered the fifth Sunday of Lent, most of the regulars at the Ground Zero Mass were Irish American. Many reported that one in four victims of 9/11 were of Irish descent while others thought there were more. I honestly did not know how many were Irish and how many were not. All I knew was that in Catholic Social Teaching we are taught to respect the dignity of all human persons – dead or alive, rich or poor, regardless of race, color or creed. Nevertheless, the week before St. Patrick's Day, many asked for some recognition of the Irish heritage of many of those who died. Kevin Flynn was the onsite representative of Local 3 from the International Brotherhood of Electrical Workers (IBEW). He reminded me that 61 union construction workers were killed on 9/11, with 17 members belonging to Local 3 IBEW. Local 3 had the most deaths of any Local of the union construction workers – not only that, but most of those 61 workers were of Irish descent.

I asked Kevin if Local 3's Pipe and Drum Band, the Sword and Light Band, would play at the March 17th Ground Zero Mass. The reasoning behind this request was that the Sword and Light Pipe and Drum Band played not only at many funeral Masses for union construction workers but also at funerals for uniformed personnel of New York City whose own pipe and drum bands were stretched thin and fatigued from playing at numerous other funeral Masses. For example they covered the New York Fire Department which lost 343 of its members). Kevin concurred with my reasons and made the arrangements.

By word of mouth during the previous week many workers, volunteers and family members of Irish descent showed up for this moving Mass. For the first time, not only was the American flag on display but the flag of the Republic of Ireland was on proud display as well. The homily was not devoted to Irish heritage but to the need for tolerance and acceptance of all God's people. We should remember the signs that read, "No Irish Need Apply." We Irish who were victims of discrimination should also be sensitive to those who may be victims of discrimination as well whether they are Protestant, Jewish, Hindu, Buddhist or, yes, even Muslim. The warped minds of the 19 Muslims who took down the Towers contrasted so strongly with that of the goodness of the overwhelming majority of Muslims worldwide. All participants understood that telling message.

HOLY WEEK – March 24-31, 2002

PALM SUNDAY – March 24, 2002

Sunday, March 24th, was Palm Sunday and the start of Holy Week. Since I was only permitted to have a 30 minute Mass, I did an abbreviated version of the Reading of the Passion. There was no homily, but instead, a long Prayer of the Faithful in which many participants often prayed aloud their particular intercession. I nearly ran out of palm for the participants but thankfully one of the worshippers brought some extra from St. Paul's Chapel. St. Paul's Chapel is located on nearby Church St. and Vesey St. It was a continued source of compassion and comfort for all people of faith during that time of hardship. They were not just ecumenical[2] but mostly interfaith in their welcoming message of hospitality.

HOLY THURSDAY – March 28, 2002

I was given permission to say a brief Holy Thursday Mass at 8 PM. There was a smaller crowd this time yet still as robust as always. I decided

---

2   Ecumenical refers to warm relations of cooperation between different churches who are not yet in union with each other, e.g., between Catholics and Protestants.

not to conduct the ritual of the washing of the feet for sanitary reasons as the ground was cool and wet but I did point out 12 particular participants, both men and women, and asked them to continue to serve one another with humility and virtue in the spirit of the 12 Apostles. The emphasis of the homily was that "we receive the Body of Christ as the Body of Christ". The Church teaches that the Eucharist is the source and summit of our faith. The word "Eucharist" means giving thanks, and we at Ground Zero should give thanks for the blessings that God has given us.

GOOD FRIDAY – March 29, 2002

Again, I received special permission to conduct an ecumenical Good Friday service. It was indeed a powerful service with over 200 participants all in their hard hats. We prayed together the Stations of the Cross with 14 different participants each reading one Station at a time with the Ground Zero Cross prominent in the background. When it came time for the 12th station where Jesus died on the Cross, I asked everyone to "Please kneel". There was complete silence except for the machinery at Ground Zero doing its own version of a Gregorian chant. I then asked them to pray aloud the names of those they knew who died on 9/11. As each name was mentioned, one could hear crying either in the voices of those providing the names or those who knelt and remembered those who died on that fateful day. To this very day, it was the most powerful rendition of the Stations of the Cross I have ever experienced in my all years of ministerial priesthood. Good Friday had new meaning for many participants that day.

The veneration[3] of the Cross centered on the steel cross that I used for weekly Mass and which was made out of the steel of W.T.C. Tower I. It was shaped and given to me by the Ironworkers of Local 40. I held the Cross and each participant, Catholic or not, came forward with a kiss of veneration. Many people cried when they kissed the Cross and blessed themselves afterwards. I then distributed Holy Communion, which was consecrated the night before at the Holy Thursday Mass. I heard a number of confessions after the service. Some had never confessed before since they were not Catholic. Others were Catholic, but had not confessed for over twenty years. I heard many confessions during those nine months at Ground Zero, with the largest number being during Holy Week and, particularly, on Good Friday. Interestingly, the next time Good Friday falls on March 29 would be 2013. That day will also be significant.

---

3   Veneration – a respect for persons or things considered holy or praiseworthy.

EASTER SUNDAY – March 31, 2002

At this Easter Sunday Mass family members of victims exceeded the number of recovery workers. It appeared that there were over 250 people for Easter. There were no Easter bonnets nor dozens of Easter lilies nor Easter bunny chocolates. Instead photos of their loved ones, the welling up of tears and the need to answer those prolonged questions. Did Jesus really rise from the dead? Will we really be reunited with our loved ones in Heaven after we die? The real question – will we be reunited someday with those whom we loved and who died on September 11, 2001? One mother of a fallen firefighter looked me in the eyes and bluntly asked me, "Please remind us about the gift of eternal life. I know it in my heart. I need to feel it in my heart again."

Believe me, the Franciscan friars provided me with a great theological education. With such complex, mind boggling courses such as eschatology[4] and soteriology[5] how could I explain the end time, Judgment Day, salvation history and the hope of the resurrection all in one homily? These family members and recovery workers were searching for meaning and an affirmation of their belief in eternal life. However, I was no St. Anthony of Padua, no St. Bernardine of Siena, no St. Clare of Assisi, and I fully admit, with all humility, I was not and am not a saint! I am a sinner with many faults and I have much to account for come Judgment Day. Nevertheless on that Easter Sunday at Ground Zero I was going to be Brian Jordan, son of Eileen Murphy Jordan and Gerard Jordan. I was a proud son of Brooklyn, raised in Long Island and a frequent visitor to the Rockaways, Queens. These areas, among the myriad of others, were greatly affected by 9/11 and the deaths of so many loved ones. I was not going to preach like a saintly theologian, but as a flawed Franciscan who happens to be a New Yorker.

I began the homily with a loud, bellowing voice proclaiming, "YES, I BELIEVE!" I continued in that vein, "If I did not believe in the gift of eternal life, I would not be here today. In fact, I would not even be a Franciscan priest. Scholarly subjects like theology and Sacred Scripture provide me with insight into the suffering and heartaches we have all felt since 9/11. I am not trying to convince you of what to believe and what not to believe. I trust you all as adults so please trust in me as to why I say I believe in eternal life." I went on for about 7 minutes, naming the loved

---

4   Eschatology – the theological study of the final form of all creation in the Risen Christ.

5   Soteriology – the theological study of Redemption or Salvation as the healing and transforming action of God among us.

ones who I knew had died and why I know, yes, *I know* I will see again. I pointed to the Cross as the vehicle of death just as the two planes were the vehicles of death for the Towers. I pointed to the 16 acre Ground Zero lot as the tomb where Jesus had lain for three days as did their loved ones. As Jesus rose from the dead so too would their loved ones rise from the dead. I provided some humorous anecdotes about what we will all do together when we meet again in Heaven. I paused and said, "So, will you be reunited with your loved ones if you really believe? I cannot tell you what I believe, but you cannot take away from my belief that the gift of eternal life is for all who believe." After the homily participants smiled and clapped. This marked the first and only time I received applause for an Easter Sunday homily. Afterwards the mother of the fallen firefighter came up to me right away, planted a kiss on my right cheek and said, "Thank you for the reminder and the inspiration. Now I know I will see my son again."

APRIL 2002

During the month of April, the Ground Zero Mass had its share of regular churchgoers and visitors from around the world who lost loved ones on 9/11. The international participants showed that they mirrored the same level of solidarity as the American people had. Both sides lost loved ones at Ground Zero and so they stood together in unison. Some people even identified themselves as atheists and agnostics. Although they decided not to receive Communion during Mass they recounted how they felt welcome and comforted at Ground Zero. Why? One atheist said, "No one made judgments on one another, it was just selfless support and compassion. Thank you." I guess whether you believe in God or not, we all need a certain degree of community support especially during tragedies like this.

MAY MASSES

MAY 5, 2002

The final tally for those who died on September 11, 2001 was near 2,900. However, it was brought to my attention by certain reliable sources that a number of undocumented immigrants were also killed in the Towers that fateful day. For a variety of reasons their names and identities may never have been recorded. I had no way of verifying the allegation but living in the most ethnically diverse city on earth I would not be surprised if many undocumented Mexicans, Chinese, Senegalese and other ethnic workers did die that day with their deaths gone unreported. Rather than forget them, one Cuban American volunteer worker, Rhonda Villamia, asked that we include in our intentions on the May 5th Mass all the unknown who may have died that day. Coincidentally, it was Cinco de Mayo, a day celebrating a Mexican victory over French forces in Mexico during the 19th century. We remembered not only Mexicans but all undocumented and unidentified persons who died on 9/11. The world may not have known who they were but Almighty God certainly knows and reveres them. We prayed for all that day known and unknown.

MOTHER'S DAY – May 12, 2002

Since the first Sunday Ground Zero Mass in April 2002, I made a concerted effort to invite mothers, grandmothers and godmothers of those who died on 9/11 to join us for a solemn Mass on Mother's Day. I offered each one a special and individual blessing. Union construction workers arranged to have a beautiful flower arrangement made for each of the mothers, grandmothers and godmothers. Unsurprisingly there were nearly 300 people who participated in this heartwarming and meaningful Mass. I gave a brief homily citing the sanctity and dignity of motherhood. I recalled the image of Michelangelo's *Pieta'* that depicts the Blessed Mother weeping over the lifeless body of her only son, Jesus Christ. Later Mary would be at the First Pentecost, the Birthday of the Church. Eventually, mother and son are united through the Ascension of Jesus into Heaven and Mary's Assumption into Heaven. I told the mothers, grandmothers and godmothers that, "Although your sons, daughters, grandsons, granddaughters, and godchildren may have died, like Mary, you will be reunited with them one day." I then gave a general blessing followed by individual blessings. The Eucharist followed after the general intercessions.

It was customary at the Ground Zero Mass for everyone to hold hands for the Our Father to demonstrate our unity within our community. What occurred while we were about to pray the Our Father was something so wonderful, so precious, that no Hallmark card could ever do it justice. Furthermore, Hollywood and Broadway could never have conceived what was about to happen. As we were about to pray the Our Father, about 20 members of the United States Special Forces came into the area to see, for the first time, the Cross at Ground Zero. They did not realize that Mass was going on, and they kept a polite, courteous distance. I asked them to join in and pray the Our Father with us by holding hands together. They reluctantly agreed to do so. After the conclusion of the Our Father, I asked them who they were and why they were here. The commanding officer identified them as members of an elite unit of US Special Forces who were about to go to Afghanistan to fight the Taliban and to find those responsible for this dastardly attack. They said they wanted to see the Cross at Ground Zero before they deployed for Afghanistan. I yelled out in the loudest voice and asked them, "DO YOU REALLY WANT TO KNOW WHAT YOU ARE FIGHTING FOR? Look at the faces of these mothers, grandmothers and godmothers who lost their precious loved ones on September 11th. You mothers, grandmothers and godmothers don't seek revenge but justice for your loved ones. Look into the faces of these brave young men who are about to go to war to fight for America." I continued, broke down in emotion, and yelled out, "YOU ALL NEED EACH OTHER! Look at each other and tell each other that you love each other. Let's offer each other a sign of peace – not a handshake, but hugs and kisses."

Oh my Lord! Never in my life, not to this very day, have I ever seen a longer, more emotionally wrenching sign of peace during a Roman Catholic Mass! This Mass was not just for Catholics but for all who suffered at 9/11. The "kiss of peace" lasted at least 7 minutes. Mothers and grandmothers were holding on tightly to these brave young men about to risk their lives for God and country. As I watched these courageous men who were about to go into battle I thought they may not have had the opportunity to say good-bye to their own mothers and grandmothers. There was not a dry eye onsite. Even the toughest cop, firefighter, and construction worker cried that day – not with sadness, but with the joy of watching the beauty of motherhood, grand-motherhood, and god-motherhood.

MAY 26, 2002

In early May, we were informed that the recovery operation would officially come to a close on May 30th. This Sunday would be the second to the last at Ground Zero, and was also the day before Memorial Day. Since members of the US armed forces would be away on that hallowed Monday, we decided to have a special Memorial Day Mass for that Sunday. Many veterans from past wars, including World War II, the Korean War, the Vietnam War, and the first Gulf War, participated and prayed for all the present members of the armed forces who were about to go to war in Afghanistan. The Pledge of Allegiance, God Bless America, and the National Anthem had special significance for us that day.

MAY 30, 2002

For me, after the Cross, the most important artifact at the site was the Last Beam at Ground Zero. The union construction workers who labored and served on four quadrants faithfully for nine months were asked to escort the Last Beam, a 30 foot steel beam, from the pit up the long ramp and back to West St. where it would be transported to Kennedy Airport for safekeeping until a proper memorial was built. This was a very meaningful evening for the union construction workers who toiled at Ground Zero. A plethora of international media attention was directed to the New York City police and fire departments in addition to the Port Authority police and rightfully so. About 80% of those who worked in the recovery operation were union construction workers. They were the ones that lost 61 members of the Building Trades. No, they were not uniform personnel, but their "physical sign" is the hardhat. They were given a budget and a time frame for the demolition and cleanup operation that ended up being done under budget and under schedule. They loved their country and felt a great sense of responsibility to finish the task with poise and professionalism. They exceeded the expectation of every construction and demolition expert throughout the civilized world.

While the beam was being hoisted up, the foreman for the task Willie Quinlan of the Local 40 Ironworkers looked on proudly at his team of volunteer construction workers. The crane operator, Harold Rochelle, of Local 14, 14-A Operating Engineers, skillfully hoisted the final beam up on top of a flatbed trailer that was driven by a resourceful Teamster 282 driver. Going up the ramp behind the flatbed truck led by the Local 608 Carpenters Union Pipe and Drum Band we were surprisingly greeted by US Marines and US Navy sailors who were in town for Fleet Week. On both sides of the ramp these Marines and sailors were applauding the union construction workers. At the top of the ramp were employees of city agencies, in particular the Department of Design and Construction led by Commissioner Ken Holden. It was also heartening to see the new Mayor, Michael R. Bloomberg, handing out personal flags to the union construction workers. These fine, patriotic, prayerful, and hard-working union construction workers have finally been given their long deserved and overdue recognition. About time they were finally appreciated!

THE LAST OFFICIAL MASS – June 2, 2002

Advance notice was given for the last official Mass by the Cross at Ground Zero. The Taj Mahal was taken down and the Salvation Army was gone. Although great efforts were still being made to recover bodies and body parts, the site was now considered a construction site in secular terms. For most of us though this was and would always remain sacred ground.

The FDNY Pipe and Drum Band volunteered to play at the Mass. The Juilliard School of Music Choir also agreed to sing. They gave the best rendition of The Battle Hymn of the Republic I have ever heard. I thanked all who participated and tried to get each agency in order. To show I was a flawed Franciscan, I forgot to mention the Operating Engineers of Local 14, 14-A and 15. Believe me, they sure reminded me afterwards with a few choice words and light punches. Hardhats!

Over 400 people, mostly family members of victims, participated in this solemn Mass. The ones who kept order were my good friends from the Port Authority Police Department, Lt. John Ryan and Sgt. Tom Kennedy. These two officers represented the very best of what law enforcement is and what it is supposed to be. Before the closing blessing I asked former Mayor Rudy Giuliani to offer some brief remarks. He did so with poise, heartfelt emotion and brevity. Say whatever you want about Rudy Giuliani he came up to the plate and he delivered not only for New York City but for the country and for the whole world. He personally attended over 200 funerals of the dead from 9/11 mostly without advance fanfare. He truly grieved and was not seeking cheap publicity as his harsh critics contended. Also in attendance was my good friend, Richard Sheirer, the former commissioner of the Office of Emergency Management, a fine public servant and a great man. My last words were, "The Mass is ended – go in peace." All responded, "Thanks be to God."

THE REAL LAST MASS – Father's Day, June 16, 2002

Even though I agreed not to say Mass on site anymore, I still went to visit the uniform services and construction workers down on Ground Zero. Most of them wanted another Mass since some of them could not attend the June 2nd Mass. After some colorful words from some of the workers and even "extremely spirited" phone calls, I agreed to say one more Mass onsite. It would be Father's Day Mass on June 16th. When I told my own father about this Mass, he insisted that he wanted to attend as well. How could I deny my own father? When I told the police and firefighters that my father had no ID to get in, they said, "Don't worry, let him be next to you and he is in." Security really got tight after June 2, 2002 for a variety of reasons (for example, property protection). It was quite difficult to let people in since I had no official authorization for this particular Mass.

For this Mass, FDNY Deputy Chief Ron Woerner assumed control. This fine firefighter took responsibility for the atmosphere at the Mass. He allowed people in and told them this was sacred ground and not a tourist trap. Reverence was displayed at this Mass. There were fewer than 50 people, but equal treatment was given to fathers, grandfathers, and godfathers. A general blessing was given, followed by an individual blessing. I intentionally chose to bless my own father last. I introduced him to the assembly after his blessing and they graciously gave him an applause. I never sought affirmation for my ministry nor gratitude. Nonetheless, it felt so satisfying to see my father recognized. Why? If it were not for him and my mother, I would never have had the rare honor to serve as a chaplain at Ground Zero and preside at these Masses. After the Mass, we all paused at the Cross. My father put his arm around me and said that he loved me. I told him that I loved both my father on earth and Our Father in Heaven.

JUNE 2002 – OCTOBER 2006

The Ground Zero Cross remained onsite near the corner of Church St. and Cortland St. until October 5, 2006. It still remained as a source of comfort and consolation for many workers and family members and friends of loved ones during that time.

CHAPTER 2

The Ground Zero Cross Moves
To St. Peter's Church

"Memory is the treasure and guardian of all things."
— Cicero, *De Oratore*, Chapter 1, Verse 5.

The Port Authority of New York and New Jersey is a bi-state government agency that has been in existence since the early 20th century. The Port Authority owned the property where the 9/11 attack took place including W.T.C. 6, where the Ground Zero Cross was found. Over the years I became very friendly with the Port Authority Police Department especially Lt. John Ryan and in particular Sgt. Tom Kennedy. Both remain close friends. I also got to know the senior Port Authority engineer on the Ground Zero site, Peter Rinaldi. Peter had a tremendous responsibility for the care of the site, and took personal interest in its rebuilding. I did not envy the arduous tasks that the Port Authority had in this rebuilding process or what career workers were being subjected to with regard to the political football that was going on among the elected officials of city, state, and federal governments.

I am neither a political pundit nor an investment banker nor do I pretend to be. That said one did not have to be a rocket scientist to ascertain that the rebuilding of the W.T.C. was going to be controversial from the start and, daresay, till the end. My close friend and confidante, Edward J.

Malloy, president of the Building Construction Trades Council of Greater New York (leader of over 100,000 construction workers) was a member of the Lower Manhattan Development Corporation (LMDC), which was responsible for the planning and financing of the new W.T.C. site. Even Ed indicated that there was considerable controversy of what to do and when to do it.

That also came to include the remaining artifact onsite – the Ground Zero Cross. Over 300,000 signatures were submitted to keep the Cross onsite even during the rebuilding process. The majority of these signatures were collected by union construction workers of New York City locals. Rumors were circulating during Holy Week 2006 that the Ground Zero Cross was going into an airplane hangar at John F. Kennedy Airport in Queens until the proposed 9/11 Museum was to open. At that point in time, no date was given on when the 9/11 Museum would become a reality.

When I asked certain members of the Port Authority if the rumors were indeed true or not, they refused to confirm or deny them. I had, and still have, immense respect for the Port Authority of New York and New Jersey. Besides losing 37 Port Authority police officers on 9/11 they also lost numerous civilian workers in the Towers. Nevertheless I was not sure if their top-level people understood that removing the Ground Zero Cross from this sacred ground would cause a tremendous uproar among the union construction workers and the family members of loved ones who continued to find great consolation by its presence. I contacted Ed Malloy and we sought a meeting with the decision makers at the Port Authority of New York and New Jersey.

HOLY WEEK 2006

Let us be honest! The so-called "Last Beam" escorted out in a solemn ceremony on May 30, 2002 from Ground Zero to JFK Airport was not the Last Beam. The actual last beam was the Ground Zero Cross. It stayed onsite until October 5, 2006! This is no offense to the enormous significance it exemplified, namely, the bravery and professionalism of all the recovery workers who served at Ground Zero for any part of the nine month recovery period. As Willie Quinlan, Local 40 ironworker differentiated, "The Last Beam is for the workers, and the Ground Zero Cross is for everyone who believed and worshipped onsite." Great distinction!

Thousands of others, besides myself, found it unimaginable that the Ground Zero Cross would be moved offsite and put in a cold, impersonal airplane hangar for storage. Had the Port Authority not grasped the meaning that this Cross gave to hundreds of recovery workers and for many who lost loved ones? Evidently not. Eventually, it was brought to my attention that the rumors were confirmed as true. Plans were underway to move the Ground Zero Cross since its present location near Church St. and Cortland St. was to be excavated to make way for a new building. Before the April 11, 2006 meeting with the Port Authority, there were two key tasks that needed to be accomplished – one by myself and the other by Ed Malloy. For my part, I approached the pastor of St. Peter's Church on Church St. and Barclay St., Father Kevin Madigan, asking him if it was possible to place the Ground Zero Cross on the outside wall of the church. Why St. Peter's? St. Peter's Church served as a temporary morgue for the first responders who died on the W.T.C. site. Furthermore, among those placed in this morgue was my fellow Franciscan, Father Mychal Judge, Fire Department chaplain ("Death Certificate Number One"), as well as Fire Department chiefs Peter Ganci, William Feehan and other first responders. Not only is it the oldest Roman Catholic Church in the history of the Archdiocese of New York, but this specific church was chosen to hold the Cross as it was the first house of God to respond to the tragedy of 9/11. For these reasons, Father Madigan agreed to house the Cross there temporarily provided he received permission from the leadership of the Archdiocese. As for Ed Malloy's part, He consulted with members of his advisory board to ensure that the Cross would remain nearby, that construction workers would work voluntarily, and that the necessary material would be donated for the Transfer of the Cross to a site that would be agreed by all.

With both tasks completed before the appointed meeting date, Ed Malloy, Father Kevin Madigan, and I met with Kenneth J. Ringler, Jr., the Executive Director of the Port Authority, in his office near Park Ave. South. Mr. Ringler was accompanied by a number of Port Authority engineers, lawyers, and public relations personnel to discuss our proposal. Said proposal was to transfer the Cross from its present site to the outside wall of St. Peter's Church on Church St. about 50 yards across from the W.T.C. site itself. Construction workers would work voluntarily to complete this transfer. A flatbed truck and all necessary materials would be donated.

After a brief, heated discussion, reason prevailed, and Mr. Ringler was convinced that such a transfer was a good idea in the long run. He clearly stated that he was acting in good faith and needed to check in with a number of people before such a decision was formalized. I thanked him for his candor and asked that this agreement be done in writing in order to avoid any misunderstanding. The next day, the Port Authority's spokesman, John McCarthy, issued a statement, "We are currently reviewing opportunities to relocate the crossed beams to a nearby location which is publicly accessible." That was formal proof that the Ground Zero Cross was not going into an airplane hangar in any airport. The union construction workers won the battle on this controversy!

("The Rev. Brian Jordan stands with Edward Malloy, President of the Building and Construction Trades Council of Greater New York in front of the cross at Ground Zero, which has been slated to be moved to a hanger at JFK airport." Appleton. Featured in an article in the New York Daily News titled "Rev. Standing Guard Over WTC 'cross' by Paul D. Colford).

In the third week of May, 2006, Ed Malloy and I received two critical letters regarding the transfer of the Ground Zero Cross and its future. This was about a month after the meeting with the Port Authority's Ken Ringler. The first letter was addressed to Ken Ringler from Gretchen Dykstra, who was then the President and Chief Executive Officer of the W.T.C. Memorial Foundation. Ms. Dykstra wrote in part on May 11, 2006, "We believe wholeheartedly that this important and essential artifact belongs at the World Trade Center site as it comprises a key component of the re-telling of the story of 9/11, in particular the role of faith in the events of the day and, particularly, during the recovery efforts. Its presentation will help to convey, with sensitivity and significance, this critical part of the story to the many visitors expected to come to the site for years to come." Ms. Dykstra later wrote, "…most likely at the World Trade Center Memorial Museum."

Honorary Board Members
George H. W. Bush
41st President of the
United States

Jimmy Carter
39th President of the
United States

William J. Clinton
42nd President of the
United States

Gerald R. Ford
38th President of the
United States

Honorary Trustees
Jon S. Corzine
Governor, State of New Jersey

George E. Pataki
Governor, State of New York

Michael R. Bloomberg
Mayor, City of New York

Rudolph W. Giuliani
Former Mayor
City of New York

Board Members
John C. Whitehead*
Chairman

Dr. Josef Ackermann
Paula Grant Berry
Sir John Bond
Debra Ballinger
Russell L. Carson*
Kenneth L. Chenault
Robert De Niro
Samuel A. DiPiazza, Jr.*
Christopher A. Hoyt
Maurice R. Greenberg
Dr. Vartan Gregorian
Patrick K. Harris
William S. Harrison, Jr.
Lee A. Ielpi
Monica Iken
Robert Wood Johnson IV
Thomas A. Johnson*
Robert Keohane
Ambassador L. Paul Bremer
Peter M. Lehrer*
Howard W. Lutnick
Julie Menin
Ira M. Millstein*
The Right Hon.
Brian Mulroney
Richard D. Parsons
Peter G. Peterson
Emily K. Rafferty
Kevin M. Rampe*
Thomas A. Renyi
David Rockefeller
Dr. Judith Rodin
Thomas H. Sayles
E. John Rosenwald, Jr.*
Jerry I. Speyer*
Anne M. Tatlock *
Daniel A. Tishman
Lieut. Bruce Wallin
John E. Zuccotti*

Gretchen Dykstra
President and
Chief Executive Officer*

*Executive Committee Member
Or Liaison

World Trade Center
Memorial Foundation

May 11, 2006

Mr. Ken Ringler, Jr.
Executive Director
The Port Authority of NY & NJ
225 Park Avenue South, 15th Floor
New York, NY 10003

Dear Ken:

     Pursuant to our recent meeting, I am writing to confirm our mutual understanding about the cross-shaped artifact at Ground Zero.

     We believe wholeheartedly that this important and essential artifact belongs at the World Trade Center site as it comprises a key component of the re-telling of the story of 9/11, in particular the role of faith in the events of the day and, particularly, during the recovery efforts. Its presentation will help to convey, with sensitivity and significance, this critical part of the story to the many visitors expected to come to the site for years to come.

     We have further explored the issue with members of the Lower Manhattan Clergy Council and New York Disaster Interfaith Services, who fully endorse our understanding that as a public institution, the World Trade Center Memorial Foundation should present this artifact in a way that tells the story of 9/11 and not as an object of veneration. As a public institution, we will not explicitly offer religious services in association with the artifact. Here again, the Clergy Council was fully and emphatically in agreement.

     We look forward to working with the Port Authority and others who care about the artifact to ensure the temporary and secure placement of it during construction on the site, and to its meaningful return to the site – where it belongs – for its eventual long-term installation, most likely at the World Trade Center Memorial Museum.

Sincerely,

Gretchen Dykstra

proof of going into 9/11 Museum

One Liberty Plaza, 20th Floor, New York, New York 10006
T 212 312 8800 F 212 312 7951
www.buildthememorial.org

The second letter was written by Ken Ringler on May 16, 2006. This letter was intended as a follow-up to Ms. Dykstra's letter, but was only addressed to Ed Malloy and myself. I was extremely gratified by Mr. Ringler's letter because he followed through with his promises from the April 11th meeting. He not only agreed to transfer the Cross to the specified location at St. Peter's Church but also ensured that the Cross would eventually go inside the W.T.C. Memorial Museum. Mr. Ringler wrote in his May 16, 2006 letter, "The Port Authority and the W.T.C. Memorial Foundation have agreed that the steel beams in cross form will be returned and permanently installed on the site once construction has been completed. We believe this is an extremely important artifact and one that will help convey to generations of Americans exactly what happened on 9/11 and its aftermath. We now look forward to working with both of you on a plan to temporarily relocate the artifact to a public space at St. Peter's Church, where it can be seen from the W.T.C. site and viewed by millions of people each year." I was as struck then as I am now that the Ground Zero Cross by St. Peter's Church could be "viewed by millions of people each year." It would be visible not just from the inside of the proposed museum but from outside as well. Ken Ringler turned out to be a good guy. I discovered later on that he was an alumnus from Siena College, a Franciscan college, in Upstate New York which is my alma mater as well. As Ed Malloy chided me, "He had no other choice!"

TRANSFER OF GROUND ZERO CROSS TO ST. PETER'S CHURCH – October 5, 2006

The original date of the transfer of the Ground Zero Cross from the W.T.C. site to St. Peter's Church was October 4, 2006 – the 5th anniversary of the original blessing on the Vesey St. and West St. site. It was also the Feast of St. Francis of Assisi, the patron saint of ecology. Unfortunately, Ed Malloy, who was crucial in these negotiations to bring the Cross to St. Peter's, was unavailable that day. As such, the date was changed to the next day, October 5, 2006 to accommodate his busy schedule.

It was a simple, solemn ceremony. Once again, Local 40 Ironworkers, led by Danny Doyle, and Local 15 operating engineers hoisted the Cross onto a flatbed truck driven by a member of the Teamsters Local 282. The truck was supplied by Bovis Lend Lease Construction Company. About 250 construction workers, family members and uniform personnel processed north on Church St. from Cortland St. up to Church St. and Barclay St. It was about six long blocks and the flatbed truck drove less than 15 MPH. When we finally got to the Church St. side of St. Peter's Church,

Charlie Vitchers, foreman for Bovis Lend Lease, skillfully re-hoisted the Cross from the flatbed truck and onto a metal foundation. The cross stood upright with a full view of the W.T.C.

Father Kevin Madigan provided a short prayer followed by remarks from Ed Malloy and Richard Sheirer, the former commissioner for the Office of Emergency Management. I blessed the Cross, as it was now rededicated by St. Peter's Church. Mark Gajewski of Local 30 Stationary Operating Engineers provided a steel plaque from Tower I which was inscribed with the words I composed – "The Cross at Ground Zero, Founded September 13, 2001, Blessed October 4, 2001, Temporarily Relocated October 5, 2006, Will Return to W.T.C. Museum, A Sign of Comfort for All" (Reviewed by Eric Konigsberg in his New York Times article titled "Brief Journey for an Icon of the Attack on New York"). The construction workers all gave a collective sigh of relief. They now had visible reassurance that the Ground Zero Cross had a new home – at least a temporary one. After the ceremony, Ed Malloy and I looked up to the Cross and we both echoed Ken Ringler's words, that by St. Peter's Church, the Cross "could be viewed by millions." That very phrase stayed with the both of us for a long time. The Cross looked quite prominent standing against the wall of St. Peter's Church right on Church St. Many would agree for the next five years.

SAINT PETER'S CHURCH – October 5, 2006 – July 23, 2011

The Ground Zero Cross looked like an authentic Cross by St. Peter's Church as it faced the W.T.C. Mr. Ringler eventually retired from the Port Authority. Ed Malloy later followed suit as he stepped down as president of the Building Trades of Greater New York. He was replaced by Gary LaBarbera, who was formerly the president of the Joint Council 16 of the Teamsters Union. It was Gary who personally arranged for the flatbed trucks to transport the Cross to its three destinations: 1) West St. and Vesey St. 2) Church St. and Cortland St. 3) Church St. and Barclay St. Gary also helped coordinate the Teamster-driven trucks that removed the debris from Ground Zero during the nine month recovery operation. He had a personal investment in the Cross not only as a member of the Building Trades but as a devout Catholic who had prayed the rosary faithfully for decades. It turned out that Mr. Ringler's words did indeed ring true – the cross was viewed from St. Peter's Church "by millions" each year.

The promise that the W.T.C. Memorial Museum would open shortly after the recovery period was not fulfilled. Political football, financial entanglements, and disagreements among various factions all led to its delay. I knew from day one that no one person or decision regarding the 9/11 Memorial Museum was going to appease everyone. It was not humanly possible. I figured it was better to be patient and not get involved in the various controversies this issue presented. Besides, the Ground Zero Cross looked quite inspiring where it was by St. Peter's.

In the early months of 2010, I was contacted by Alice Greenwald, the executive director of the National 9/11 Memorial Museum, for an informal meeting at her office near the W.T.C. site. Alice was the founding director of US Holocaust Museum in Washington D.C. She appeared to have an excellent resume and was deemed capable by many to help organize and institute "a historical memory" of the experiences of 9/11. In the same office, I also met other people I knew from my Ground Zero experiences such as Ron Vega from the Department of Design and Construction who sang the best rendition of "Danny Boy" at the Ground Zero Masses I ever heard. It was a treasured memory because it was Ed Malloy's favorite song. There was Lou Mendes who used to work with Ron at the DDC. Lou was now in charge of construction at the 9/11 Memorial Museum. They and others must have told Alice of my devotion to the Ground Zero Cross. She was prepared and asked me a series of intelligent questions about regarding my experience with the Cross. Alice was uncertain when the Cross would be transferred to the Memorial Museum as there was still "a cloud of unknowing" as to when the museum would be ready to open. As Ed Malloy said to me, "Nothing comes easy in New York politics!"

EPIPHANY – June 2010

In early June 2010, while standing in front of the Ground Zero Cross, Ed Malloy, Gary LaBarbera, and I experienced what you would call an "epiphany of Biblical proportions". In ten minutes we watched at least 150 passersby stop and gaze at the Cross. They either prayed to the Cross or took pictures. The Cross had profound meaning for them because it *looked* like a Cross. An "epiphany" means... Hallelujah! Did we three have an epiphany simultaneously? Why don't we have a meeting with the Museum officials and the pastor at St. Peter's Church and lobby them to keep the Cross at St. Peter's Church? We were sure they would agree to that proposal.

Boy, were we wrong! On June 29th, 2010, a meeting was scheduled between the officials of the Memorial Museum, Gary LaBarbera, Ed Malloy, and myself to discuss the possible transfer of the Cross. We met again with Alice and members of her staff together with the president of the 9/11 Museum, a lawyer named Joseph Daniels. The three of us presumed that his job was to raise funds for the Museum and to meet with public officials. He admitted that he had no experience with museums but would respect what transpired on 9/11. For our part, Gary, Ed, and I shared our belief that the Cross would be best served by remaining at St. Peter's Church. This revelation came as a great surprise to the Museum officials but they all indicated that they understood our feelings and beliefs regarding this request. Mr. Daniels did state that he personally hoped the Cross would be a part of the Museum. We then agreed to have another meeting in the summer to discuss the matter once more. This next meeting would be later on in the summer. Gary, Ed, and I left the meeting hoping that the Ground Zero Cross would remain by the outside wall of St. Peter's Church.

RECONSIDERATION OF THE GROUND ZERO CROSS GOING INTO THE W.T.C. MEMORIAL MUSEUM

I still feel then as now that the Cross should have remained on-site by St. Peter's Church. Unfortunately the first indication this would not happen came on the afternoon of August 2, 2010 when I received a curt, unambiguous phone call from Alice Greenwald. She stated that she was calling on behalf of Mr. Joseph Daniels, her boss, and that she was instructed to say that the "Cross is the property of the Memorial Museum given to it by the Port Authority and should be returned to the Museum whenever the proper time takes place on the planning schedule." So much for the polite discussion during the June 29th meeting! I told Alice that I was shocked and dismayed for a variety of reasons. First, why was it that Joe Daniels could not call me personally, rather than sending you to me? Secondly, my colleagues and I never knew that the Cross was the legal property of any group including the Museum. Thirdly, I vividly recall stating, "Alice, I hope you and the Museum are not threatening legal action. If you are, please be prepared to explain why you would do so!" After the phone call, I immediately called Gary LaBarbera and Ed Malloy to tell them what had transpired. Both recommended that we meet with the Museum officials as soon as possible.

On August 9th, Gary LaBarbera and I met with the Museum officials in their office. Ed Malloy could not attend the meeting so instead I asked my good friend Richard Sheirer, former commissioner of OEM, to attend the meeting. Although Richard favored bringing the Cross to the Museum he indicated that he had an open mind. Alice Greenwald led the meeting with her staff and also invited Father Kevin Madigan of St. Peter's Church to participate. I found it very interesting that Joe Daniels was not at the meeting but Father Madigan was! Alice politely stated that she understood our concerns but reminded us that the Cross was given to the Museum by the Port Authority since the beam itself was part of the building property of September 11, 2001. I found it noteworthy that the opportunity to provide such documentation for this argument was never presented at this meeting nor any subsequent meeting. I thought to myself, *Are they bluffing or do they have something in writing?* Father Madigan reminded me that at the April 11, 2006 meeting, the Cross would have only temporary space at St. Peter's since he and other church authorities promised an artist that a different Cross-like object would be given to St. Peter's Church. Furthermore, he stated that he did not want to renege on that promise. Given the importance of the Ground Zero Cross one of my colleagues took offense at this rationale. I objected that the drawings given to us of the Ground Zero Cross did not look like a Cross. If the Cross were to go into the Museum we ask for assurances that the Cross would look like a Cross just as it presently does. The Museum officials and even Father Madigan agreed to that request. Again I asked that this be put in writing. I now knew what the strategy of the Museum officials was – let Father Madigan do the heavy lifting and keep Joe Daniels out of harm's way. But it was not yet checkmate. I immediately thought of another move to advance the cause of the Cross.

On August 16, 2010, I sent a fax letter to Archbishop Timothy M. Dolan, the new spiritual and canonical leader of the Archdiocese of New York. Archbishop Dolan had only been the archbishop for 14 months and was still on a ministerial learning curve. The good, jovial archbishop was not there on 9/11, and was not expected to fully grasp the pain and suffering on that day. Nonetheless from his talks and conversations he appeared to be sensitive to the issue. I wrote to him requesting in writing that the Cross either be kept at St. Peter's Church or at least that he help me amplify the visibility of the Cross if it was to go into the Memorial Museum. I also requested a face-to-face meeting or at least a meaningful conversation. Neither occurred as I was given no response to the fax letter at all. I presumed that since it was summertime he might have been on vacation.

The Most Reverend Timothy M. Dolan, STD, DD
Archbishop of New York
Archdiocese of New York
1011 First Avenue
New York, New York   August 16, 2010

Your Excellency,

   Greetings. I am respectfully requesting a face to face discussion or some quality
phone time concerning the Cross at Ground Zero presently located at St. Peter's
Church on the corner of Church and Barclay Sts. A controversy is simmering and
I would like to resolve this matter quietly rather than engage in a public debate!

BACKGROUND The Cross at Ground Zero was discovered by a union construction
worker on Sept. 13, 2001. I presided over a formal blessing ceremony on Oct. 4,
2001. The Cross was relocated on Ground Zero property at the corner of Church
and Cortland Sts. On Feb. 14, 2002. After a hotly contested debate, a compromise
was reached in which the Cross was transferred to St. Peter's Church on Oct. 5,
2006. It was verbally agreed and a letter was presented by the WTC Memorial
Museum to invite the Cross to be part of the Memorial Museum upon its
completion. The WTC Memorial Museum has requested the transfer of the Cross
to the Museum come mid October of this year. What has occurred is a
reconsideration by Father Brian Jordan, the Executive Board of the union-based
Building and Construction Trades Council led by Gary LaBarbera; Edward Malloy
of the New York State Building Trades and many union construction workers who
had served at Ground Zero. Why the reconsideration? Because the Cross looks like
a Cross in its present site at St. Peter's Church. After examining the visuals for the
location of the Cross in the proposed site it does not look like a Cross but a mere
artifact! It does not need to be said that this Cross has given sacred comfort
through the years! It is more than an artifact, it is a sign of God's presence!

PRESENT STATUS We have had two meetings with the WTC Memorial Museum,
the last being Aug.9 in which Fr. Kevin Madigan participated. Gary LaBarbera,
Edward Malloy, Richard Shierer and I all presented the views of the building
trades, the Cross does not look like a Cross in the proposed Memorial Museum. The
building trades prefers to leave it at St. Peter's Church. Fr. Madigan said he made a
promise to a benefactor when Cardinal Egan was Archbishop. That would mean,
The Cross at Ground Zero will have to go in the near future. None of us want a
battle with Fr. Madigan but we do want increased prominence of the Cross IF it is
to go to the Memorial Museum. I do have some constructive ideas to resolve this
matter behind the scenes. This is the reason I request a conference with you .

                    Sincerely,

                Father Brian Jordan, OFM

Meanwhile both Gary LaBarbera and Ed Malloy shared their support for keeping the Cross at St. Peter's as there were no written assurances from Museum officials that the Cross would receive a prominent position in the Museum and not get lost in the shuffle. Finally, a sign of hope seemed to have arrived! Immediately after the September 11, 2010 Labor Day Mass in St. Patrick's Cathedral, Gary LaBarbera and Ed Malloy met with Archbishop Dolan and pleaded for the Cross to remain by St. Peter's Church. I was not present at this particular Mass due to a funeral at a different location. According to both Gary and Ed who never lied nor exaggerated to me Archbishop Dolan seem to voice and nod his approval by embracing both their shoulders – a common gesture of the Archbishop. A few days later, on September 16, 2010, I sent another letter by mail to the Archbishop asking him to keep the Cross at St. Peter's since he'd already given verbal approval to my two trusted colleagues and friends. Part of my September 16, 2010 letter read, "Gary LaBarbera informed me that he raised the point with you after the Labor Day Mass on September 11, 2010 in front of other labor leaders. He received the distinct impression that you also favor keeping the Cross at St. Peter's. If that is true, I am gratified and relieved. We should keep the living sign of our faith for all the People of God to see and not hide our lamp of faith under bushel baskets."

Thos Most Reverend Timothy M. Dolan, STD
Archbishop of New York
Archdiocese of New York
    1011 First Avenue
New York, New York   Sept. 16, 2010

Your Excellency,

   Greetings.   Last month on Aug. 16, I sent a fax to you concerning the Cross at
Ground Zero which is presently located at St. Peter's Church on the corner of
Church and Barclay Streets. Your secretary informed me that he placed it in your
desk for review. I am not sure if you have seen it as of yet. Nevertheless, since
Aug.16 much activity has occurred. The rank and file of the union construction
workers plus their own Executive Board and Council of Delegates have strongly
asserted that they very much prefer to keep the Cross at St. Peter's rather than
going underground to the World Trade Center Memorial Museum where they
believe will be lost among many other artifacts.

   Edward J. Malloy of the NYS Building and Trades Council and Gary LaBarbera
of the NYC Building and Trades Council and I have met with the management of
the Memorial Museum and voiced our concerns that the Cross should presented as
a Christian Cross within a prominent place. We have yet to receive a satisfactory
response. We hear excuses and that a museum is not a church. They do not want
to favor one religion over another. My response is that over 2100 of the 2800
victims killed on 9/11 were either Roman Catholic or Christian. The Cross was
discovered by a union construction worker and many people to this very day find
great comfort in the Cross. After a careful period of reflection, I fully concur that
the Cross should remain at St. Peter's Church and should continue to serve as a
Christian Cross above the ground and outside rather than be lost among artifacts
underground and inside.

   Gary La Barbera informed me that he raised this point with you after the Labor
Day Mass on Sept.11, 2010 in front of other labor leaders. He received the distinct
impression that you also favor keeping the Cross at St. Peter's. If that is true, I am
so gratified and relieved. We should keep the living sign of our faith for all of the
People of God to see and not hide our lamp of faith under bushel baskets!

              Sincerely,

              Father Brian Jordan, OFM

Unfortunately the Archbishop's written response of September 29th, 2010 was hardly a "lamp of faith." In fact, it was a disappointment for Gary, Ed, and me. Evidently the Archbishop had reconsidered which was clearly his prerogative. He wrote that after he reread my fax letter and mailed letter he conferred with Father Kevin Madigan, the pastor of St. Peter's Church, about this sensitive issue. Father Madigan advised the Archbishop that the Ground Zero Cross should go into the Museum since he made a promise to another artist to put an artistic-designed Cross (not found at Ground Zero) in the exact location where the Ground Zero Cross was at St. Peter's. What disturbed and confused me most was the Archbishop's explanation why the Cross should go into the Museum and not at St. Peter's Church. The Archbishop wrote, "While there is no intention to display the Cross in a specifically religious setting the museum officials have assured Father Madigan that it will be appropriately displayed within the context of what faith meant to those involved in the World Trade Center." That is not what I requested in the August 9th meeting in the museum office. Even Father Madigan agreed with both Gary LaBarbera and me that *if* the Cross were to go into the Museum it would occupy a prominent position. That is not what Gary LaBarbera and Ed Malloy heard from the Archbishop after the September 11, 2010 Labor Day Mass. Again, the Archbishop has the right to reconsider what he said earlier. I have certainly experienced a reconsideration of my desire to keep the Cross at St. Peter's. However had Archbishop Dolan agreed to keep the Cross at St. Peter's Church, the oldest Catholic Church in the Archdiocese, that would have been a game-changer. It would have ensured the legacy and the prominence of the Ground Zero Cross by the W.T.C. site and "viewed by millions of people each year."

PLANNING THE TRANSFER OF THE CROSS TO THE MEMORIAL MUSEUM

Well, as the saying goes, "you can't win them all." After nine years of fighting to keep the Ground Zero Cross from being buried in a landfill in Staten Island or being dispatched to a cold, dusty airplane hangar in JFK Airport I had a winning track record as the unofficial guardian of this sacred artifact! I guess the law of averages meant I would have to lose sooner or later. I agree to lose gracefully as a humble Franciscan which is not easy for a native New Yorker!

I have no personal animosity towards the Archbishop nor Father Kevin Madigan of St. Peter's Church. In fact, I have the utmost respect for Father Madigan because he was on the front lines during 9/11 and performed wonderful follow-through ministry afterwards. He went through tough times and I will always remember that he served with humble faith and unshakable trust in God. St. Peter's Church will not only be remembered for being the temporary morgue after 9/11 but as the cherished, temporary home of the Ground Zero Cross for nearly five years.

In early October 2010, I received a phone call from Alice Greenwald requesting a meeting for the possible transfer of the Cross to the Memorial Museum. Evidently, she must have heard from another source that the Cross would now officially go into the Museum. I had a long talk with Richard Sheirer who convinced me to go to the meeting with an open mind. He grabbed my arm, looked me in the eye, and said, "Hey, listen, it is not *your* Cross, Father! It happens to be the Cross of the People of God." He then smiled and hugged me. "Come on, call Gary and let's set up a meeting." I also received many phone calls and emails from family members and recovery workers asking about what was happening with the cross. I had an obligation to them as well. Richard was right, it is not my Cross – it was the Cross of the People of God. It will go into the Museum – for now.

I called Gary and he agreed to be part of the meeting. Along with Richard Sheirer, Gary and I met with Alice Greenwald and a large contingent from the Museum office including Joe Daniels who did not seem to have a worry in the world. For the sake of the common good of the People of God, I was cordial towards him but I did ask that if he had a question for me in the future please call me directly rather than going through Alice Greenwald. He agreed to do so in his own way of course via emails.

Alice ran a good meeting and recommended we plan ahead for a simple, solemn transfer ceremony. We agreed to conduct the transfer ceremony in the summer 2011, but did not nail down a specific date until another meeting was to take place. In a very friendly tone of voice I asked if I could get in writing that the Cross would be located in a prominent place. They heard me and responded with a smile. To this day I never received anything in writing as to how this Cross would be located other than a vague, non-specific drawing. I figured myriads of lawyers for the Museum had input to answer my request which was NADA – nothing! As a brave soldier of Christ my mantra said this was not my Cross but the Cross of the People of God. So let's make the best of it, show some class, and be altruistic rather than the perennial feisty Franciscan.

After a series of phone calls with Gary LaBarbera who was in contact with the Building Trades and Joe Daniels by email we agreed in the spring of 2011 that the transfer ceremony would take place in Liberty Plaza on Saturday morning, July 23, 2011. A vast amount of preparation would be involved in this simple, solemn ceremony. Mr. Daniels graciously asked me to conduct a short, meaningful, interfaith prayer ceremony which I agreed to do. I contacted Frank Silecchia and many of the workers and family members in order to inform them of the ceremony and to have them attend. Richard Sheirer agreed to contact Rudy Giuliani and Joe Lhota since they were both instrumental in saving the Cross from demolition during the first month of the rescue and recovery period. I went to confession and received spiritual advice from my confessor. I stated that I have been angry with all this tension and commotion surrounding the Cross – emotions that have been prevalent within me for ten long years. I proclaimed that I wanted to be reconciled from this anger and harsh demeanor and be at peace. I wanted to find some sense of closure as the unofficial guardian of the Cross. After this ten year odyssey, my spiritual journey with the Ground Zero Cross appeared to be coming to an end. At least I thought that was the end.

CHAPTER 3

American Atheists' Lawsuit:

To Be Or Not To Be

"Lift high the Cross, always and everywhere. I think it is the most beautiful Cross I have ever seen and it was never commissioned, designed or paid for unless in deep human tragedy."

— Father Kevin Tortorelli, O.F.M.,
Liberty Plaza, July 23, 2011.

Saturday morning, July 23, 2011, was the date that all parties agreed to have the ceremony of the Transfer of the Cross from St. Peter's Church to Liberty Plaza by Church St. and Liberty St. The ceremony began around 10 AM. The Cross was removed from the side of St. Peter's Church and placed securely on a flatbed truck which was led by a police escort from both the New York City Police Department and the Port Authority Police. I rode along in the truck together with Local 580 and Local 40 ironworkers down Church Street towards Liberty Plaza.

With the help of a crane, the cross was raised from the truck and held in an upright position on the corner of Liberty Plaza facing the World Trade Center site. At exactly 10:30 AM (the same time as when the Ground Zero Masses began) I began a brief interfaith ceremony in front of 300 people. Most of those attending were the union Building Trades workers who served at Ground Zero while other workers involved at the site were also present including FDNY, NYPD, sanitation workers, Port Authority police, and even some PA engineers. Some family members of victims also participated. Among the participants were former Mayor Rudy Giuliani, Gary LaBarbera, Frank Silecchia, the former Local 731 laborer who found the Cross, and my good friend Richard Sheirer, the former OEM commissioner. Then there took place the blessing with Holy Water and Prayer: four blessings in each direction as I did on October 4, 2001 – North, South, East, and West.

TRANSFER AND BLESSING CEREMONY OF THE WORLD TRADE CENTER
CROSS, JULY 23, 2011 AT 9:30 AM TO ITS FINAL HOME—THE WTC MUSEUM

A. THE BLESSING CEREMONY WITH HOLY WATER AND PRAYER

1. FIRST BLESSING "GIVE PRAISE TO OUR CREATOR, GOD THE FATHER, WHO CREATED HEAVEN AND EARTH. GOD THE FATHER IS THE FATHER OF ABRAHAM WHO IS FULLY EMBRACED BY JUDAISM, CHRISTIANITY AND ISALM. WE ARE SISTERS AND BROTHERS OF THE SAME GOD THROUGH SHALOM, SALAAM AND PEACE. BLESS ALL THEIR RESPECTIVE MEMBERS WHO DIED HERE ON SEPT. 11, 2001"

2. SECOND BLESSING "GIVE PRAISE TO OUR REDEEMER, GOD THE SON, WHO WAS FULLY HUMAN AND FULLY DIVINE. JESUS CHRIST DIED FOR OUR SINS AND ROSE FROM DEATH FOR OUR SALVATION. THE OVERWHELMING NUMBER OF THOSE WHO DIED ON 9/11 WERE CHRISTIAN, ESPECIALLY ROMAN CATHOLIC. BLESS THE LOCAL CHURCHES WHO GAVE WITNESS THAT FATEFUL DAY—ST. NICHOLAS ORTHODOX CHURCH THAT WAS DESTROYED AND SOMEDAY TO BE REBUILT; ST. PAUL'S CHURCH THAT PROVIDED OUTSTANDING HOSPITALITY FOR MANY; AND ST. PETER'S CHURCH THAT SERVED AS A TEMPORARY MORGUE AND THEN HOST FOR OUR CROSS FOR THE PAST FIVE YEARS. BLESS OUR CHRISTIAN ECUMENICAL MISSION."

3. THIRD BLESSING "GIVE PRAISE TO OUR SANCTIFIER, GOD THE HOLY SPIRIT WHO HAS SUSTAINED US IN PATIENCE AND PRAYER . 50 DAYS FROM TODAY, WE WILL HUMBLY RECALL THE TENTH ANNIVERSARY OF SEPT. 11, 2001. IN THE SPIRIT OF PENTECOST WITH THE VARIOUS LANGUAGES AROUND THE GLOBE, LET US REMEMBER ALL THE NATIONS THAT LOST LOVED ONES ON 9/11. ALTHOUGH, THEY MAY HAVE WORSHIPPED BUDDHISM, HINDUSIM, SHINTOISM AND OTHER FAITH TRADITIONS FROM THEIR FARAWAY HOMELANDS; THEY ARE CLOSE IN OUR HEARTS NOW AS ALL ARE WHO DIED ON THAT DAY AND LEFT MANY LOVED ONES. WE ALL SHARED GRIEF—MAY WE ALL COMFORT ONE ANOTHER AS SISTERS AND BROTHERS THROUGHOUT THE WORLD!" BLESS OUR GLOBAL INTERFAITH MISSION!"

4. FOURTH BLESSING " AS THE PEOPLE OF GOD, WE WILL TRY TO LIVE IN PEACE AND HARMONY AS PROMISED IN THE DECALOGUE OF ASSISI"

Decalogue of Assisi for Peace

On January 24, 2002, religious leaders from around the world gathered in Assisi, Italy. They included Pope John Paul II and a number of Catholic cardinals; Bartholomew I, spiritual leader of all Orthodox Christians; a dozen Jewish rabbis, including some from Israel; 30 Muslim imams from Iran, Iraq, Saudi Arabia, Egypt, and Pakistan; dozens of ministers representing Baptists, Lutherans, Anglicans, Methodists, Presbyterians, Pentecostals, Disciples of Christ, Mennonites, Quakers, Moravians, The Salvation Army and the World Council of Churches; and dozens of monks, gurus and others representing Hindus, Buddhists, Sikhs and Zoroastrians and native African religions. Their meeting culminated in a commitment to peace adopted by all present. It is called the "Decalogue of Assisi for Peace."

1. We commit ourselves to proclaiming our firm conviction that violence and terrorism are incompatible with the authentic spirit of religion, and, as we condemn every recourse to violence and war in the name of God or of religion, we commit ourselves to doing everything possible to eliminate the root causes of terrorism.

2. We commit ourselves to educating people to mutual respect and esteem, in order to help bring about a peaceful and fraternal coexistence between people of different ethnic groups, cultures and religions.

3. We commit ourselves to fostering the culture of dialogue, so that there will be an increase of understanding and mutual trust between individuals and among peoples, for these are the premise of authentic peace.

4. We commit ourselves to defending the right of everyone to live a decent life in accordance with their own cultural identity, and to form freely a family of his own.

5. We commit ourselves to frank and patient dialogue, refusing to consider our differences as an insurmountable barrier, but recognizing instead that to encounter the diversity of others can become an opportunity for greater reciprocal understanding.

6. We commit ourselves to forgiving one another for past and present errors and prejudices, and to supporting one another in a common effort both to overcome selfishness and arrogance, hatred and violence, and to learn from the past that peace without justice is no true peace.

7. We commit ourselves to taking the side of the poor and the helpless, to speaking out for those who have no voice and to working effectively to change these situations, out of the conviction that no one can be happy alone.

8. We commit ourselves to taking up the cry of those who refuse to be resigned to violence and evil, and we are desire to make every effort possible to offer the men and women of our time real hope for justice and peace.

9. We commit ourselves to encouraging all efforts to promote friendship between peoples, for we are convinced that, in the absence of solidarity and understanding between peoples, technological progress exposes the world to a growing risk of destruction and death.

10. We commit ourselves to urging leaders of nations to make every effort to create and consolidate, on the national and international levels, a world of solidarity and peace based on justice.

Included in the July 23,
interfaith cere

In an interview I had with Catholic News Agency reporter Kevin J. Jones, he wrote, "The World Trade Center cross is still a 'sign of comfort to many people' says a Franciscan priest who describes himself as the unofficial guardian of the Ground Zero Cross. Also, 'it's a sign of consolation and comfort for those who lost loved ones… For the dead, the cross signifies the death of Jesus Christ. It also gave hope and support to the living, especially the rescue and recovery workers, the firefighters, police officers, construction workers and many others.' Furthermore Jesus is both the victim and the victor of the cross. Despite the cruelty of his death, Jesus is also the victor of the Resurrection, of life over death" (Jones, Kevin J. Personal interview. July 29, 2011).

After the blessing ceremony, the Cross was again placed on a flatbed truck and driven into the World Trade Center construction site. It was then hoisted up by a crane and skillfully deposited inside the National 9/11 Memorial Museum. After fighting for this Cross for nearly ten years, I believed this odyssey had finally come to an end and that the Cross was in its rightful home. Such was my mindset on that record breaking 100 degree morning, July 23rd. I thanked all involved especially Rudy Giuliani and Richard Sheirer.

THE AMERICAN ATHEISTS ASSOCIATION LAWSUIT

Monday, July 25, 2011 was my 56th birthday. I thanked God for the gift of life. I also thanked my parents, Eileen and Gerard, for their cooperation in God's gift of Creation that brought me into the world. Birthdays are meant to be for celebration. My 56th birthday ended in commiseration.

Early that afternoon, I received a phone call from Richard Sheirer. He indicated that he had heard from a reliable source that a "particular group" of atheists was suing the Memorial Museum and other entities for a allowing a religious object such as the Ground Zero Cross to be part of the Museum. According to them, it was a "clear violation of church and state". He was not yet sure whether or not I was included in the lawsuit. For once I was speechless and flabbergasted! How could this group of atheists do this? I never met them nor heard of their complaint beforehand! God must have a sense of humor! It was 100 degrees when the Cross went inside the 9/11 Museum – now myself and others were about to face intense legal heat.

A couple of days later, Richard called again and verified that the defendants in the lawsuit were the National 9/11 Memorial Museum, the Port Authority of New York/New Jersey, the Lower Manhattan Development Corporation, the Governors of both New York and New Jersey, and the mayor of New York City, Michael Bloomberg, who is also chairman of the 9/11 Museum. Last but certainly not least both the Church of the Holy Name of Jesus in Manhattan and I as the only individual were included in the lawsuit. I was shocked and dismayed that not only was I sued but also my church of residence. The Church of the Holy Name of Jesus had absolutely nothing to do with the Cross at Ground Zero. I did relay this fact to an attorney who was handling the case for this atheist group. The attorney asked me who had authorized me to bless the Cross at Ground Zero – my immediate reply was, "Almighty God asked me to bless the Cross. Will you sue God as well?" Evidently, that person was not satisfied with my answer, so they included the Church of the Holy Name of Jesus anyway.

When I was finally served through the mail in August 2011, I read the names of the plaintiffs and did not recognize a single one. Not only that but I had never met any of them before. I had no idea that they were upset. Why didn't they have the decency to tell me to my face? At the very least they could have written me, emailed me, or called me about their alleged "pain"! Had I been given the opportunity I would have gladly sat down with them and listened to their concerns. I would have told them that many atheists attended the Ground Zero Masses. They may not have believed in God but they were still very much welcome to be part of that healing community during the Masses. Not one atheist ever reached out to me personally to convey deep dissatisfaction with the Cross during that near ten year period. In general, I have no problem with atheists. I respect their right not to believe in what I do believe but I most certainly expect that they would in turn respect my right to believe and worship.

MEDIA SUPPORT

Apart from a few media outlets I was gratified by the overwhelming amount of newspaper editorials, radio spots, blogs, and TV interviews that favored keeping the Cross in the 9/11 Museum and that were deeply critical of the American Atheists lawsuit. A "trinity" of meaningful editorials were of great significance to me.

According to experts, the New York Daily News is the most read paper in New York City. What was important to me was that during the first few months after the October 4th, 2001 blessing of the Cross, the Daily News printed a depiction of the Ground Zero Cross as a template on top of each page that covered 9/11 related stories. I am so grateful to the Daily News for their imagination and sensitivity in printing that Ground Zero Cross depiction. On hearing about this frivolous lawsuit the Daily News wrote in an insightful editorial on July 29, 2011 titled "Atheists' lawsuit against displaying Ground Zero cross at 9/11 museum is insane." The editorial stated that, "In the days since 9/11, this cross has filled many, mourning hearts with some small measure of hope and faith and calm. And now a group of atheists wants to rip that away... It is an argument as galling as it is childish... The argument is downright delusional." I found their final lines to be the best ones, "Perhaps this is a headline grabbing stunt to raise the profile of a guerilla group of nonbelievers. We hope and pray that is the case. No one could be so stupid as to believe this complaint has merit" (Editorials).

Susan Jacoby, a blogger for the Washington Post, author of many insightful books and an atheist, wrote the second editorial. She is sensible, intelligent, and honest in her writing, and has easily become one of my favorite "spiritual" authors. Consider her August 1, 2011 blog post that was printed in the Washington Post entitled, "Atheist group's frivolous lawsuit aims to bar "cross" from 9/11 museum." She writes, "This suit not only misconstrues the First Amendment but detracts from the seriousness of many genuine violations of the separation of church and state that have become embedded in our society." She continues, arguing that:

We are talking about history, albeit quite recent history, and the fact that some firefighters and mourners seized on this piece of metal as an object of veneration does not remove it from history. The object... is part of what New Yorkers lived through. It is not a statement of government endorsement of Christianity. (Jacoby)

Susan criticized this as a "meaningless lawsuit" as she states, "What I find dismaying about lawsuits of this kind is that they make it more difficult to focus public attention on real and serious violations of the separation of church and state." She concludes by writing that:

The American Atheists clearly subscribe to the notion that all publicity is good as long as they spell your name right... But the press will pounce on the story of the American Atheists trying to exclude a battered, cross-shaped piece of metal from a museum precisely because such wasted gestures confirm negative stereotypes about atheists. (Jacoby)

I found her writing, and this editorial specifically, to be quite persuasive, as it came from one of the most respected writers in the country – one who just happens to be an atheist.

The editorial in the August 9, 2011, issue of the Washington Post was one that I found to be quite astute and convincing in its argument. An excellent excerpt from this editorial about the Cross includes:

To omit it from the National September 11 Memorial and Museum – as a misguided lawsuit seeks to do – is tantamount to ripping out a page of history... [The lawsuit] argues that the cross, a symbol of Christianity, has no place in a museum that is on government property and receives some government support, though it is run by a private foundation. (Editorial)

The Washington Post editorial asked the best rhetorical question – "Does anyone really think that this museum was built for the express purpose of displaying the cross? Or that no secular significance attaches to the steel beams that became part of the landscape of Ground Zero?" To this day, the American Atheists Association has never adequately answered those masterful questions. The Washington Post answered those penetrating questions itself with the closing sentences used in this stirring editorial:

The cross is as historically important as the smashed New York City firetruck that will go on display or the flagpole from the world Trade Center. Yes, it is a powerful symbol of faith to some but that should not banish it from a museum that will give tribute to the very American attributes of freedom and tolerance that the Sept. 11 attackers sought to destroy. (Editorial)

I appreciate and would like to thank the Washington Post for also reminding readers that the 9/11 tragedy was not exclusively tied to New York City. It was an incident that involved the destruction of a portion of the Pentagon. It was only due to the efforts of those brave, daring passengers on United Flight 93 that prevented the attackers from destroying another national shrine.

One of my fellow friars at St. Francis of Assisi on West 31st St. in Manhattan, Father Andrew Reitz, O.F.M., brought to my attention another publication that wrote about the Cross going into the 9/11 Museum and the subsequent lawsuit. I must admit that I do not read this publication often. Nonetheless, the Aug 10-17, 2011 edition of *L'Osservatore Romano*, the Vatican's leading newspaper, was an eye-opener; the article was titled, "The Cross at Ground Zero a symbol of hope." It reiterated the fact that the Cross was inserted into the 9/11 Museum on July 23, 2011 and made mention of the frivolous lawsuit. Earnestly, I truly am appreciative of how they included quoting my words at the July 23rd ceremony: "The cross is a symbol of consolation and comfort for those who lost loved ones, but it also gave hope and support to the living, especially the rescue and recovery workers, firefighters, police officers, construction workers, and many others." Most Franciscans toil in the front lines of the ministerial down and dirty. When they saw my picture in the leading Vatican newspaper, I was the focus of friendly, derisive comments for quite some time.

DIVERSE SUPPORT

Atheists, agnostics, and those who believe in God are all protected under the First Amendment. I respect anyone else's right not to believe in God in private or in public. However, the American Atheists Association unwisely crossed the line for two distinct reasons. They are not only trying to block an artifact from going into to a museum, but they are attempting to inhibit my right to worship and bless objects in public. Though I do respect their liberties, please, either now or in the future, do not impede *my* religious liberty or any other religious minister's liberty to believe.

Besides the outpouring of support of my fellow friars of Holy Name Province, I received many letters, phone calls, emails from many people around the country upon their learning of the lawsuit – not only from Christians but also those from the Jewish faith as well as Muslims, Buddhists, and other religious denominations. In fact I received some heartfelt notes of support from some atheists who attended services at the Ground Zero Masses. They echoed the claims of many atheists that the American Atheists Association is only a miniscule fraction of atheists in the U.S. They absolutely do not represent the overwhelming majority. I say this because I never believed this was a contentious feud between Christians and atheists. I have atheist friends and colleagues and we all respect each other. Heck, even my doctor is an avowed atheist and I trust him infinitely. So help me God!

UNEXPECTED ALLY

On August 18, 2011, the Church of the Holy Name of Jesus and I received an interesting email from an individual we would never in our wildest dreams thought would approach us. She was a legal assistant for the attorney in Wyoming representing the American Atheists Association. This occurred 24 days after the lawsuit was filed publicly. It was a message of apology for her involvement in the lawsuit. This was one of the most endearing, humbling, heartfelt, and welcome emails I have ever received.

She indicated that she recently moved to Wyoming and that she needed money to help her with the transition. At first, she was grateful for the job – until this lawsuit came along, that is. She writes, with emotional and spiritual pain:

Anyway as her paralegal, I became part of an action which I felt was wrong from the get go. Nonetheless I followed instructions and orders to research, edit, etc. matters connected to the Atheists' complaint. I was appalled you and your parish were included as defendants in the Complaint. I was completely uncomfortable with association with the Atheists group and felt the Atheists were 'way out there' in whining about the placement of the WTC Cross in the memorial museum – especially since it brought comfort to many and has 9/11 history. This courageous, faith filled woman continued her wise insights by saying, "…but my guilt in participating in that lawsuit brought about much angst and was in part why I needed to get away from that place."

She quit and found another job. She concluded with such a plea I won't soon forget: "Please accept my apology to you and to the Holy Name of Jesus Parish. May Christ be with you. I am hoping for forgiveness…" I read and re-read that email over and over again. Even to this day my eyes still well up with tears when I reflect on how touching her words were. I felt from the beginning that this lawsuit would go nowhere. Even so I was still so moved that this brave Christian woman stood by her beliefs and principles and left that environment in search of other employment. I hope and pray she was successful.

LEGAL REPRESENTATION

Evidently, the American Atheists Association didn't have a problem only with the Cross in the National 9/11 Memorial Museum. They took issue with a Roman Catholic priest of the Franciscan Order blessing objects in public. They were messing with the wrong Franciscan. We Franciscans prefer reconciliation over litigation. We would rather work things out face-to-face than engage in legal battles. Unfortunately, this particular group of people lacked the intestinal fortitude to reconcile. They preferred litigation over reconciliation. They never even bothered with mediation! They sued me, a Ground Zero priest, for exercising my God-given duties to bless people and bless the Cross. Well, this son of Brooklyn was ready, able, and willing to respond in the best way possible. I was going to listen to sound, legal advice.

Sent: Thu, Aug 18, 2011
Subject: Apology to Father Brian Jordan, O.F.M. and Holy Name of Jesus Parish of NYC

Dear Father Jordan,

After I accepted a job as a paralegal in a law firm in the humble town of Green River, Wyoming, three days into working there, the attorney which I worked under,   accepted an assignment to draft and file a Complaint on behalf of American Atheists. I was out of a job since I relocated to Wyoming (following my husband's relocation) for a year, and was so happy to gain employment in a law firm (an arena where I worked for over 18 years).

Anyway, as her paralegal, I became apart of an action which I felt was wrong from the get-go, but nonetheless followed instructions and orders to research, edit, etc., matters connected to the Atheists' Complaint. I was appalled you and your parish were included as defendants on the Complaint; completely uncomfortable with associating with the Atheists group; and felt that the Atheists were "way out there" in whining about the placement of the WTC cross in the memorial - especially since it brought comfort to many and has 9/11 history.

Slightly over three weeks into working there, I resigned my new position. Admittedly, my departure was mostly based on the very heavy, dark and negative environment there, but my guilt of participating in that lawsuit brought about much angst and was, in part, why I needed to get away from that place.

Please accept my apology to you and Holy Name of Jesus Parish. May Christ be with you. I hoping for forgiveness, I am,

Very truly yours,

[Names omitted for privacy.]

I reached out to a number of lawyers and judge friends who encouraged me to choose a lawyer who would represent me and the Archdiocese of New York (which owned the property of the Church of the Holy Name of Jesus). They advised me that both the Church and I should be represented by the same lawyer so that both parties can be dismissed from the lawsuit. I agreed to their advice. After discussing the issue with the local pastor of the Church of the Holy Name of Jesus I called the chief counsel of the Archdiocese of New York. He agreed to choose a lawyer who would represent the Church, the Holy Name of Jesus and me. I was greatly relieved and thankful when he provided me the name of this lawyer who I heard had merited many positive comments as a fine lawyer. Yet for some inexplicable reason another official from the Archdiocese office got involved and selected a different lawyer without informing the chief counsel at the time. To this day I am not sure why this change was made. I was quite pleased with the original selection.

The new lawyer called me in late August 2011, and said that he was assigned to represent both me and the Church of the Holy Name of Jesus. Remarkably he did not know himself why he was selected. The pastor of the Church of the Holy Name of Jesus and I were not asked to sign a letter of agreement nor any other written document with this lawyer. I thought that was strange. I presumed that when a lawyer represents an individual or an institution some type of written agreement is made by both parties for their protection.

So now a new chapter in the saga of the Cross was about to happen – a fight to keep the Cross in National 9/11 Memorial Museum. I read about other lawsuits by certain atheists groups that were somewhat successful in blocking religious objects from being placed in public places. However, this was a nonprofit museum! Could they really succeed in restricting religious objects from going into a museum? By Labor Day weekend, 2011, I called both Gary LaBarbera and Ed Malloy and told them I wish the Cross had stayed at St. Peter's Church or at least in some other outdoor setting in a place of prominence. Ed Malloy had advised me previously in an August phone call, "Well, it should have stayed where it was but that is water under the bridge. Fight for the Cross to stay in the 9/11 Museum and hope it will be placed in a prominent space."

COUNTERSUIT OR NO

In September of 2011, some colleagues from Ground Zero asked me if I was willing to consider a countersuit against the American Atheists Association. They argued that my First Amendment right to exercise my priestly ministry was being attacked by this lawsuit. At the outset, I was a bit confused. If as Franciscans we believe in reconciliation over litigation then if I agreed to a countersuit I would be just as bad as the atheists' group themselves. On the other hand I had never heard of a religious minister who sued by atheists countersued on behalf of the First Amendment. My gut reaction was not to proceed. My conscience though was asking me if I was avoiding a potentially worthwhile fight, viz., to fight for the First Amendment rights of religious ministers in the future.

In November 2011, I asked my Franciscan religious superiors about the possibility of a countersuit. They took some time to deliberate. They got back to me and indicated that they preferred the Franciscan tradition of reconciliation over litigation. They discouraged me from proceeding to a countersuit. In religious orders, the vow of obedience can determine public actions such as a countersuit. I understood their concerns but my conscience was still not yet clear on the issue.

In December 2011, I went to my doctor for my annual physical and told him of my ethical dilemma concerning the lawsuit with the American Atheists Association. He has been my doctor for over a decade. In fact, he was the one that gave me one of the best pieces of advice I needed in order to lift some of the fog surrounding my conscience. He instructed me to stay away from a countersuit because I would only help supply another reason for them to get into the newspapers. He told me that this small group does not represent the majority of atheists in the U.S. He concluded:

"All this sad group wants is cheap publicity. Do not give them any more fuel for their fires of disillusionment. You and I are both protected by the First Amendment. They will eventually discover that when the judge makes the final decision. I repeat, this particular group does not represent all atheists in the U.S."

The other excellent bit of guidance came from my fellow friar and ordination classmate, Father John Coughlin, O.F.M. John not only holds a canon law degree from the famous Gregorian University in Rome, but also a civil law degree from the prestigious Harvard University Law School. He is also an adviser to the United States Conference of Catholic Bishops. He has been a professor of law and theology at Notre Dame University and is currently associated with New York University Law School. John and I started out together as prospective Franciscans in 1977. We knew each other very well and I trusted him completely with those pangs of conscience on this issue. He carefully read the atheists' lawsuit and spoke with the lawyer for the Archdiocese of New York who represented me and the Church of the Holy Name of Jesus. He took the matter very seriously and offered a Franciscan perspective on the matter.

John asserted that the lawsuit does not directly attack my right as a religious minister. Its primary focus was the Cross at Ground Zero. I was included in the lawsuit because I blessed the Cross in a public ceremony. John believed the lawsuit was misguided. It was not a matter of the separation of church and state because the Museum is not associated with the state – it is a nonprofit organization not run by it. My possible countersuit may be considered as legally baseless. Therefore he advised against a countersuit.

Rather than a countersuit John suggested that as a victim of a frivolous lawsuit I should be in contact and in solidarity with other religious groups and individuals around the country who have also been victimized by intimidating lawsuits. "Let us learn from both our Catholic Social Teaching and organized labor", he said. "If we come together in solidarity as religious entities not only can we respond to future lawsuits, we can also prevent them due to our combined strength with dialogue and legal resources." Sage advice from my fellow friar and priest.

DEATH AND FUNERAL OF RICHARD SHEIRER

On the night of January 18, 2012, I had a long talk with my dear friend and confidante, Richard Sheirer. He consoled me about this troubling lawsuit and offered some keen observations about the legal and political implications of this vexing issue with the atheists. We said goodbye to each other as we hung up the phone. The next day, I received a heart-pounding email message from retired FDNY firefighter Bill Hayes: "I regret to inform you that our dear friend Richard Sheirer died today in Beth Israel Hospital. May he rest in peace." I was completely devastated. I said to myself three times, "I can't believe it!" I burst into tears and prayed to God to take care of the best Jewish friend I ever had.

After calling Richard's wife Barbara, I discovered that Richard was experiencing chest pains while driving to work from his home in Staten Island. Richard had the presence of mind to drive himself to Beth Israel hospital. He was admitted and later died from complications of the heart and lungs. He had a pre-existing medical condition. I had the unique honor of preaching at Richard's funeral service at the well-known Temple Emanu-el Synagogue on 5th Ave. on Sunday, January 22, 2012. Other prominent rabbis and a priest also shared reflections at the service. The most memorable part of the funeral service took place when Richard's five sons came to the pulpit and gave five brief, poignant reflections about their wonderful father – Matthew, Joseph, Christopher, Andrew, and Paul honored their father with words of true justice in his memory.

What am I going to do now without Richard? He was one of the greatest advocates of the Cross. He was present at every Transfer Ceremony and at the last official Mass at Ground Zero on June 2, 2002. I lost not only a great friend but a consoler, ally and real inspiration to carry on. At his funeral service I vowed to ensure that Richard's contribution to the National 9/11 Memorial Museum would be showcased. Why do I say that? Richard and I are from Brooklyn. Each of us was born a Doubting Thomas – we'll believe it when we see it. But I am being selfish! Barbara, a devout Catholic and her five sons also raised Catholic, lost far more than I did. I acknowledge that reality of family ties. Even so he was such an enormously monumental figure in my life. I still have a prayer card with Richard's photo on the night stand by my bed. Each night as I did on January 18, 2012 I say "Good night Richie" and turn off the light to go to sleep.

CHANGE OF LAWYERS

The new lawyer assigned to me and the Church of the Holy Name of Jesus by the Archdiocese of New York was a competent attorney but he appeared to be very busy and his primary focus appeared to be was his practice and the Archdiocese. I felt that he did not have my concerns as his priority. As a case in point, I gave the attorney and his staff all the documents, correspondences, and emails concerning the Cross. They only gave the attorney representing the atheists the May 11, 2006 letter from Gretchen Dystra of the 9/11 Memorial Museum and the May 16, 2006 letter from Ken Ringler of the Port Authority about agreeing to transfer the Cross into the 9/11 Memorial Museum when it was to open. I asked why they did not include my fax letter of August 16, 2010 and my September 16, 2010 letter to Archbishop Dolan requesting that the Cross remain at St. Peter's Church. In addition why didn't they provide the Archbishop's response letter of September 29, 2010 in which he reconsidered his position and took the view that the Cross should not remain at St. Peter's? His office replied that it was not applicable to the case and not necessary to give to the lawyer representing the atheists. I responded that it was indeed pertinent and that it would have been a game-changer if the Archbishop actually agreed to keep the Cross at St. Peter's Church. First and foremost, there would have been no lawsuit by the American Atheists Association and, secondly, it would have retained its place of prominence outdoors where no one would have to pay to see it.

They completely ignored my request and reiterated that it was not relevant. I no longer felt that I was being heard. It seemed like all they wanted to do was to have me and the Church of the Holy Name of Jesus dismissed from the lawsuit. That was certainly their main goal but I wanted more because this was a teachable moment to respond not only for this lawsuit but for others in the future. Although many lawyers told me afterwards that the legal strategy of the Archdiocesan lawyer was correct it reminded me of the fact that the entire legal dispute could have been so easily avoided if the Cross had remained at St. Peter's Church. Even now, I still believe I was right.

In early February 2012, the lawyer for the Archdiocese informed me that both I and the Church of the Holy Name of Jesus were dismissed from the lawsuit by Federal Court Judge Deborah Batts. I expressed my gratitude and thanked them for their efforts. While I finally had their attention I also told them that I was seeking new legal counsel and signing on a letter of engagement with a new law firm in Washington D.C. – Wiley Rein LLC. Thank you and good-bye! I agreed to sign this letter of engagement as it provided both expectations and boundaries to our ability to work together legally. Besides, it was also pro-bono[6] for which I was very grateful because as a true Franciscan I was flat broke.

WILEY REIN LLC

There were two things I really enjoyed about signing on with Wiley Rein. First, they began as a law firm in the same year I was ordained to the ministerial priesthood – 1983. Second, their address is 1776 K St. NW Washington. How patriotic! Talk about unity between church and state. There it was.

The real reason I agreed to representation by Wiley Rein LLC was due to the presence of one of their brilliant lawyers Matthew Dowd. Matt was born and raised in Bayside, Queens, New York. He attended both Regis High School (a Jesuit institution) and William and Mary in Williamsburg, Virginia. If one undergoes the grueling, extremely competitive admissions process and is approved for Regis High School the students pay no tuition. Matt was brilliant from the get go and excelled not only there but in William and Mary as well. He decided he would rather be a lawyer than a scientist. So he attended and graduated from George Washington Law School. He met his wife in Washington D.C. and eventually they decided to marry. They have three beautiful children.

How did we meet? Matt was among the many lawyers who called me at the Church of the Holy Name of Jesus to offer me pro-bono legal assistance as a defendant in the case brought by this specific group of

---

6   Pro-bono – for free.

atheists. What made his call more endearing than the others was that he too grew up in a parish in the Diocese of Brooklyn. Furthermore he came from a loving, middle class family. Like myself Matt lost close friends because of the events of 9/11. Not only was He intelligent he was especially sensitive and keen to what I was going through as a chaplain and unofficial guardian of the Cross at Ground Zero. After speaking with him a couple of times he gained my trust and I enjoyed listening to his legal opinion on this lawsuit. He opened my mind and heart to the complexities of this case and to other lawsuits by different atheist groups who were against religious institutions and attempts to put religious objects in public places. The lawyer hired by the Archdiocese took great care of the Archdiocese. Matt Dowd took great care of Father Brian Jordan and other religious ministers who may be sued in the future.

A couple of times during the fall of 2011, I met with Matt in his office at 1776 K St. NW Washington D.C. At one point, He introduced me to one of his colleagues Megan Brown who was another brilliant lawyer carefully monitoring this lawsuit against the inclusion of the Cross into the 9/11 Museum. Megan Brown impressed me quite a bit. She had briefed cases before the U.S. Supreme Court. As such I thought to myself just in case this lawsuit goes that far she may be the attorney to make that argument. Furthermore she believes that there are too many frivolous lawsuits in the court system. Sooner or later the court system needs to purge itself of these senseless suits because it ties up the system with "waste, fraud, and abuse." In addition she asserts that penalties should be considered against inane cases in the future. Amen to that!

Even though I was dismissed from the case, Matt Dowd informed me that the lawyer for the American Atheists Association wanted to subpoena me for a deposition. This deposition would be videotaped and could last seven hours. Matt was concerned about this possible deposition for two reasons. First, the lawyer for the atheists was quite a character and might ask me some tough, provocative questions in order to trip me up and say things that I may regret. Secondly, as he knew and I fully admit, one of my character flaws is my fiery Irish temper. If this lawyer for the American Atheists Association tried to wear me down with excessive and offensive questions I might do something all parties would lament. In other words it was ill-advised for me to go through a deposition.

When I was served through with mail with a deposition subpoena I immediately gave the papers to Matt. He explain that the subpoena may not have been properly been served and did not provide enough time to sit for deposition. When he discovered that I would be out of the country during the requested time he composed a written legal document to both the lawyer for the atheists and to the court to remove me from a deposition. In the document he stated the importance of my trip to Northern Ireland and that I could not attend the deposition as demanded. Despite the anticipated protest by the atheists' lawyer, the district court agreed to Matt's request and removed me from the requirement of the deposition. My trip to Northern Ireland was a great success and I thought often of my good friend Ed Malloy each time I heard "Danny Boy", his favorite song.

DEATH AND FUNERAL OF ED MALLOY

After I returned from Northern Ireland in early May 2012 I paid a visit to Ed Malloy in his apartment in the East Side of Manhattan. For nearly a year Ed was suffering from complications of asbestos poisoning that had been in his system from his early years as a steamfitter in Local 638. He looked tired, but was greatly concerned about the future of union construction workers in New York City. He also asked about the lawsuit over the Cross and again said it should have stayed along the wall of St. Peter's Church. After our conversation I blessed him with holy water and gave him a warm embrace. I never thought that would be the last time I would see Ed Malloy alive.

In the morning of May 15, 2012, Ed Malloy died at home next to his lovely wife Marilyn. He was waked in Frank Campbell Funeral home on Madison Ave. – one of the most prestigious funeral homes in New York City. His funeral Mass was on May 18, 2012, at St. Patrick's Cathedral and was filled with all the leaders of the Building Trades union, private company owners, developers, and elected officials. What impressed me most was the huge turnout of rank and file union construction workers. They all knew that Ed started out like them – a hardhat construction worker who labored long hours to provide for his family and who went on strike against unjust working conditions and inadequate pay. Ed was one of them, and their large numbers showed they greatly appreciated him. Marilyn and their two daughters, Anne and Theresa, also valued their presence.

I remember Ed Malloy for the myriad of good deeds he has done throughout the years. I hope the public will remember and treasure the wonderful negotiation tactic he employed during our April 12, 2006 meeting with the Port Authority led by Ken Ringler. Had he not done so the Ground Zero Cross would have been consigned to a dusty airplane hangar at JFK. Who knows if it would ever have gone into the 9/11 Memorial Museum? I cannot fathom that I lost two of my closest advisers and supporters of the Ground Zero Cross within four months of each other. I now have Gary LaBarbera and the Building Trades union members to help carry out the message of the Ground Zero Cross.

MAY 2012 – MARCH 2013

While awaiting a decision from Federal Judge Deborah Batts of the Southern District about this lawsuit I began to research with keen interest other institutions around the country that were being sued by various atheist groups for their alleged role against the separation of church and state. I do have a right to bless objects in public and could not comprehend why the American Atheists' Association sued me personally in their contemptible lawsuit. I was not being sued for money. However if I were to lose I would incur the legal costs of both my lawyer and regrettably the atheists' lawyer! What!? I took a vow of poverty. I have no money to spend on the atheists' lawyers! Through this research, I was now sensitized as to what other religious groups and individuals were going through around the country.

I became familiar with various legal groups who reached out to different individuals, small towns and institutions who were the subject of trivial lawsuits by atheists. I am grateful for both the American Center for Legal Justice run by Jay Sekulow, the Becket Fund for Religious Liberty and other groups who provide free legal counsel for those groups who are being sued for trying to place significant religious objects in the public square. Although the lawsuits by the atheists are by and large flippant, they are meant to be intimidating to those groups and individuals who like myself have little or no money to defend themselves without legal counsel. This is where I agree with Megan Brown's thesis that judicial means need to be employed to prevent these frivolous lawsuits from jamming up the legal system in the U.S. and penalties need to be incurred by any individual or group who consistently file such crazed lawsuits. Intimidation is part of the bizarre strategy that select atheist lawsuits employ when they prefer litigation over reconciliation. Their strategy is to weaken religious-minded people almost immediately with the introduction of a lawsuit and its inherent costs. In the words of St. Paul, "it is when I am weak that I am strong." Being willing to stand up to this method of intimidation is my new motto!

GOOD FRIDAY – March 29, 2013

On Good Friday, March 29, 2012, the Communion and Liberation Group, a lay-run Catholic community, organized a Way of the Cross from St. James Cathedral in north Brooklyn to St. Peter's Church near the World Trade Center. This was the tenth anniversary of this evocative Way of the Cross. Hundreds of devoted Christians processed from the Cathedral of St. James across the Brooklyn Bridge. They passed by City Hall, Wall St., and finally, the World Trade Center on Church St. to St. Peter's Church. It was amazing to witness the Crucifixion of Jesus Christ from the oldest church in the Diocese of Brooklyn (St. James) to the oldest church in the Archdiocese of New York (St. Peter's). This tradition of the Way of the Cross on Good Friday has been an annual liturgical event each year since 2002 and was inspired by the events of 9/11.

As the new chaplain for St. Francis College in Brooklyn, I recruited a number of students to join the procession for the Way of Cross on Good Friday, March 29, 2013. It was heartwarming to see so many young people join with adults in crossing over the Brooklyn Bridge in prayer and song as we recalled Jesus carrying his instrument of death towards Calvary. After we passed by City Hall and on the way towards the World Trade Center it dawned on me that this date March 29th was very familiar. The last time Good Friday fell on March 29th was in 2002, when I conducted Good Friday services at Ground Zero in front of the multitude of construction workers, police officer, firefighters, Salvation Army volunteers, sanitation workers, and family members! Is this a coincidence or was this meant to be a sign given by Almighty God?

As I passed by Ground Zero on Church St. I thought of the mass murder that occurred on September 11, 2001. I thought of all the people sentenced to death without a trial, warning, or any valid reason. This was their Calvary and I wanted to pray for them and remember them with sincere love. We arrived at St. Peter's Church at about 3 PM and I simply gazed at the World Trade Center site in prayer. For some reason, I experienced a quiet sense of relief – it was as though a burden had been lifted from my shoulders. I felt at peace and I wanted more of that feeling of peace in my life.

I decided to go back home to my new friary, Our Lady of Peace, in the Gowanus section of Brooklyn. When I returned to the friary my fellow friars who served there, Fathers Patrick Boyle, O.F.M. and Orlando Ruiz, O.F.M., had just completed the Good Friday services in the parish church. They were joined by three other friars of the Immaculate Conception Province who were visiting from their friary in Lower Manhattan. They were Father Primo Priscitello, O.F.M., Father John Scarangello, O.F.M., and Brother Ron Bolfeta, O.F.M. It was about 5:15 in the afternoon when we sat down around the dining room table sharing pizza and salad. Suddenly, I received a text message from Matt Dowd – it was one of the most poignant text messages I have ever received in my life. It read: "Congratulations! Judge Batts ruled in favor of the Cross in the 9/11 Memorial Museum." I immediately yelled out aloud, "THANK GOD!" When my fellow friars asked me what had happened I gladly informed them of the contents of the text message from Matt Dowd. They all smiled and congratulated me for the success I earned from this long journey of protecting the Cross. Not only that, but the date and time of this significant decision by Judge Batts was not lost on them. They all expressed both amazement and gratitude that this decision was released on Good Friday. We all raised our glasses together and praised God. Later when I talked to Matt by phone he estimated that the decision regarding the Cross was released by the office of Judge Batts around 3 PM – the exact time we Catholics believe Jesus died on the Cross! Furthermore, that was around the same time I received that wonderfully calm wave of peace when I stood by St. Peter's Church after we had finished the Way of the Cross. How amazing can it get?

The next day, March 30th, was Holy Saturday. Matt called to say that the American Atheists Association were disappointed not only by the decision itself but by its timing. Coincidentally the American Atheists Association was apparently celebrating the 50th anniversary of its founding in a national convention. From my perspective, this court decision finally proved what author Susan Jacoby, the New York Daily News and my atheist doctor were saying all along, namely, that this lawsuit "was delusional." I did not gloat over this decision. I was simply relieved and thankful. I am eternally grateful to God for being part of the Way of the Cross organized by the Communion and Liberation Community on Good Friday, March 29, 2013. The fact that two opposing groups could be celebrating a part of their history is quite ironic, no? Was this a coincidence? Humbly speaking, I do not think so.

As Matt Dowd and I expected, the lawyer for the American Atheists Association was authorized to file an appeal to the Second Circuit Court of Appeals in Manhattan a few months later. Meanwhile, I received many messages of congratulations from the construction industry in New York City both union construction workers and contractors. Among them was an owner of a scaffold company, York Scaffolding Company based in Long Island City, Queens. The owner, Ken Buettner, perhaps summed things up best when he wrote me in an email on April 3, 2013, a couple of days after the decision, saying:

"Those who do not recognize the presence of a greater being have that right but it cannot be allowed to infringe on my right to believe in God. Our founding Fathers were careful not to bind our fledging nation to any organized religion but they were also cognizant that some form of deity was at work and that they acknowledged him in their written and spoken words."

And so, the odyssey of the Cross marches on.

CHAPTER 4

Court Of Appeals Upholds
Judge Batts' Decision

"Friends show their love in times of trouble, not in happiness."

– Euripides.

THE AMICUS BRIEF – FRIEND OF THE GROUND ZERO CROSS

We had successfully cleared the first hurdle of the court case but there was at least one more court case to go -- the U.S. Court of Appeals for the Second Circuit. Matt Dowd explained the process to me by which an appeal is made to a higher court after a Federal judge makes a ruling. In this case Judge Deborah Batts of the District Court for the Southern District of New York made the ruling in favor of the Ground Zero Cross going to or staying in the 9/11 Memorial Museum. The plaintiffs, the American Atheists Association, authorized their lawyer to file a notice of appeal which they did in April 2013. Then the lawyer for the 9/11 Memorial Museum would acknowledge that motion for an appeal to the Second Circuit Court of Appeals which is located in downtown Manhattan practically walking distance from the World Trade Center. The appeal is then assigned to a panel of three Federal judges at the Second Circuit Court to hear oral arguments from all sides. Some months later, the Court would hand down a written decision for the American Atheists Association as plaintiffs, the 9/11 Memorial Museum as defendants, and the general public. Matt predicted that this appeals case would not be heard until early spring 2014.

During the late summer of 2013, Matt asked me if I would like to file an *amicus brief* in support of the Ground Zero Cross remaining in the 9/11 Memorial Museum. In layman's terms, an *amicus brief* is a legal argument to support a particular position during the appeals court process. In this case, I would be a friend, or *amicus*, of the Ground Zero Cross remaining in the 9/11 Memorial Museum. I told Matt that I needed to think and pray about it. I put the matter to prayer and spoke with my spiritual director who advised me to follow my conscience. I then decided to talk about it with my fellow friar priest, Father John Felice, O.F.M., and he greatly encouraged me to follow through with the amicus brief by saying, "Brian, we have to stand up for religious liberty. Fight the good fight".

The real moment of decision on whether or not to write an *amicus brief* came on the evening before I was to meet Matt Dowd and Megan Brown in their office on 1776 K St. in downtown Washington, D.C. This was in early September right after Labor Day weekend. I took a walk around the U.S. Capitol and as I did many times before I gazed upon the bright golden doors of the south entrance. On the left hand side, there is a depiction of a group of Franciscan friars from Spain accompanying the explorers from Columbus's second voyage to the New World. They brought the Catholic faith with them to the New World – to the Americas. If they could travel that far to bring the faith with such zeal who am I a fellow friar not to go continue on with this journey with the Ground Zero Cross? The next morning I met with Matt and Megan and shared that story with them. By all means let's go forward with the *amicus brief!* I never wrote an *amicus brief* before, but then again I was never sued before either.

AMICUS BRIEF SUBMITTED AFTER THE FEAST OF ALL SOULS

I have a confession to make. I did not author that *amicus brief* alone. Matt Dowd wrote it and was assisted by Megan Brown and Brendan Morrissey. All I did was help supply personal information, names, dates and help organize a chronology of events of the evolution of the Ground Zero Cross. With all their other responsibilities Matt and his colleagues were successful in crafting an outstanding *amicus brief.* On the Feast of All Souls, November 2, 2013, they sent me the final copy to proofread. For about two hours I carefully prayed over it. I was not making any grammatical nor content corrections. I was praying for all the poor souls who died on September 11, 2001, against their will at the World Trade Center, the Pentagon, and at the plane crash in Shanksville, Pennsylvania. I prayed that I was not only going to be the friend of the Ground Zero Cross but of the faithfully departed on this Feast of All Souls.

On November 15, 2013, Matt Dowd faithfully submitted the *amicus brief* in the United States Court of Appeals for the Second Circuit. Weeks later Matt called me to say that the lawyer for the American Atheists Association attempted to block my *amicus brief* from being entered into this appeals process. The three judge panel rejected this effort and permitted my *amicus brief* to enter the Federal record. This meant that the three judge panel would read my *amicus brief* as well as others ahead of the oral arguments which were to be held in early spring, 2014.

In late January 2014, Matt called me and said that the oral arguments for the case would be heard on Thursday morning, March 6, 2014, in Room 1703 at the Thurgood Marshall Court House, on 40 Centre St., Foley Square in downtown Manhattan. He strongly encouraged me to be present in my Franciscan habit and said he would try to be present as well depending on his work schedule. So there it was. March 6, 2014, the day after Ash Wednesday, would be the day I would finally meet the leaders of the American Atheists Association. I would finally meet the people who sued me for blessing an object in public, one of my constitutional rights. I would look them in the eye and simply ask them, "Why?"

At the same time, I was really not looking for a confrontation. That is the streetfighter in me, and I could not let that dominate me that day. Remember, Brian Jordan! You are a Franciscan first. We prefer reconciliation over litigation. Litigation might be America's favorite pastime but don't strike out in anger. Throw out the first pitch with love. Reconcile with one another says the Lord!

ORAL ARGUMENTS IN THE SECOND CIRCUIT OF APPEALS

After conducting the 10 AM Ash Wednesday services in the chapel of St. Francis College I asked those attending please to pray for me since I would be attending a Federal Appeals Court hearing the next day, March 6th, in Foley Square. I reminded the worshipers that in July 2011, a host of institutions, elected officials and I myself were sued by an atheist organization for supporting the introduction of the Ground Zero Cross into the National 9/11 Memorial Museum. Although I was removed from that ridiculous lawsuit the atheists continued their suit against the National

9/11 Memorial Museum. In the first round of litigation Judge Deborah Batts ruled on Good Friday, March 29, 2013, in favor of the Museum. As such the Museum could keep the Ground Zero Cross for public display as part of the history of 9/11. Immediately afterwards the same atheist organization filed an appeal. The oral arguments for this appeal were to be held on March 6, 2014, the day after Ash Wednesday. Furthermore, the symbolism between Holy Week 2013 and Lent 2014 was something I took note of almost immediately.

After my Ash Wednesday 10 AM service concluded at 10:30 AM (there's symbolism everywhere!), Professor Susan Saladino, head of the Department of Nursing at St. Francis College raced up to me and said, "You are not going there alone! I am going to get the nurses from a nearby hospital, nursing students, and myself to join you tomorrow. Where is this court house?" she demanded. I was truly moved by this offer since Matt Dowd could not attend. I gave her directions to the Thurgood Marshal Court House in downtown Manhattan as well as the time the appeals court would sit. Although I was gratified by Professor Saladino's offer I concluded it would be impossible for her to gather so many people in less than 24 hours.

The next morning, after an early Mass in Our Lady of Peace Parish in Gowanus, Brooklyn, I took the subway to downtown Manhattan and walked up the steps towards Foley Square. The first thing I saw was a row of TV cameras interviewing a few members of the small atheist organization who had filed the appeal. Let me just repeat that they were described to me as a small group that did not represent the viewpoints of all atheists in America. There were about twelve atheists there. That was it. After two and a half years, I was finally seeing face-to-face the very people who sued me on my birthday, July 25, 2011. I could have been angry, but all I felt was pity for them. They looked haggard and lost. I thought, *these people are responsible for all this unnecessary pain and sorrow? God forgive them.* Some of them were protesting aloud, "Put the Cross back at St. Peter's Church! That is where it belongs. You should have kept it there in the first place!" I heard those phrases expressed to the media at least three times. I mused to myself, *if you guys only knew that not only did I agree with you at one time but so did many more people who served at Ground Zero for nine months.* I then entered the court house to await the hearing, sitting by myself in court room 1703 at 9:28 AM. I had not heard back from Professor Saladino so I assumed she and her students would not be present.

Well, ye of little faith! Was I wrong! Exactly two minutes later at 9:30 AM, Professor Saladino and 15 of her students both past and present sat next to me, behind me, and in front of me in the court room for this pivotal case. The nurses and nursing students were young, energetic and thoughtful. They truly cared and were genuinely interested in what this appeals case was all about. I was overwhelmed with joy and relief. Their presence, prayers, and support were extremely touching. God has been with me during the 12 plus years I spent fighting for and protecting the Cross. I have never been alone at all over those many years, and I was certainly not alone in the crucially important appeals hearing.

The oral arguments in the appeals court began with the lawyer representing the appellants, the American Atheists Association. Up next was the lawyer representing the National 9/11 Memorial Museum who was provided equal time with his argument as to why the Cross at Ground Zero should remain in the Museum. Lastly, the lawyer for the American Atheists Association is given time for a short rebuttal of the oral argument of the lawyer for the 9/11 Museum. The three judge panel consisted of the presiding Judge Reena Raggi along with Judge Gerald Lynch and Judge Denny Chin.

Although I am not a lawyer I was surprised to see how disorganized the lawyer for the American Atheists Association, Edwin Kagin, was for this hearing. He strayed from the main issues at hand and seldom gave direct answers to the intelligent and penetrating questions proposed by the three judge panel. In great contrast, the pro-bono lawyer for the National 9/11 Memorial Museum, Mark Alcott, counsel of Paul, Weiss, Rifkind, Wharton and Garrison LLP, was clear and succinct in his oral argument to keep the Cross in the Museum. He convincingly stated that religion was part of the historical experience of 9/11. This was one of the same points I made in my *amicus brief* to the court. As such, after considering that fact, the Cross can be labeled as an artifact that is and should remain in the Museum. He then brilliantly asserted, "The Museum is neither a proponent nor opponent of religion. It is neutral." Furthermore, he contended that the Ground Zero Cross is an artifact that was discovered on site as a direct result of 9/11 and that the atheists' request to insert a plaque concerning atheists should not be included in the Museum because it was not a historical artifact found at the 9/11 site.

The total presentation of the appeals panel lasted about thirty minutes. Throughout the presentation, it seemed clear to me that the judges were strongly skeptical of the atheists' legal arguments. As the oral arguments concluded one of the judges on the panel said that they would deliberate over these arguments and legal briefs and then hand down a decision in a few months. While exiting for the elevators I overheard some of the atheists' sympathizers groan aloud, "I think we are going to lose a second time!"

HEALED AT LAST

When I left the Federal court house building I immediately thanked Professor Saladino, the nurses and nursing students for their presence and support. I thanked them for healing my wounds. When Professor Saladino asked me what wounds I was speaking of I told her that I was not referring to the physical wounds that nurses often tend to -- whether or not their patients believe in God -- but rather the spiritual wounds of bitterness and resentment I was carrying ever since I was unfairly sued by a small group of extremist individuals who did not represent all the well-intentioned atheists in our nation.

That meaningful day after Ash Wednesday I was truly healed by the insightful questions of the three judge panel of the U.S. Court of Appeals of the Second Circuit, the reliable and consistent legal advice from my pro-bono attorney, Matthew Dowd of Wiley Rein, and especially, by Dr. Saladino and those fine nurses from St. Francis College. As I reflected after the oral arguments, the Cross at Ground Zero provided comfort and consolation to both family members of 9/11 victims and to the recovery workers who served at Ground Zero for nine months and more. Without my realizing it these fine nurses provided me with that same comfort and consolation by their simple presence and the amount of concern they displayed. I thought of the term coined by Joel Osteen, "Be better, not bitter." I was bitter for a long time because I had been sued. Any priest being sued in this country has grave, negative connotations in the public eye. However this lawsuit against me was different. I am probably the only priest in the country proud to be sued for something he truly believes in – the Cross at Ground Zero.

I believe it is no coincidence that a district court federal judge issued her decision on Good Friday, March 29, 2013, to keep the Ground Zero Cross within the National 9/11 Memorial Museum. In addition, it is no accident that the Appeals Court heard oral arguments on the day after Ash Wednesday, 2014. What a wonderful Lenten season it was! At the time, I hoped and prayed that the judges of the Second Circuit would issue their decision by Pentecost, the Birthday of the Church, June 8, 2014. What fortuity or perhaps symbol of faith that would have been! Praise to God if that would have happened! Unfortunately, it did not happen.

STANDING OR NO STANDING

On June 19th, 2014, Matt Dowd called me to say that a new legal request was made by the three judge panel who heard the oral argument at the Second Circuit Court. Rather than making a decision based on the appeal itself the three judges were considering an issue that had been raised in an *amicus brief* submitted by the Becket Fund for Religious Liberty. This brief challenged whether the American Atheists Association lawsuit even had legal "standing" to challenge the placement of the Cross in the Museum. For an individual to have standing to sue there must be some concrete harm suffered by the individual. Sometimes, the courts will conclude that mere disagreement with government action is not enough. The standing requirement keeps every "Tom, Dick, and Harry" from filing suit every time a government official makes some decision. The judges demanded a maximum 15 page response from both the atheist plaintiffs and the Museum to prove that they indeed had standing. Furthermore, the judges wanted to have it in their hands by July 14th.

UNITED STATES COURT OF APPEALS
FOR THE
SECOND CIRCUIT

At a stated term of the United States Court of Appeals for the Second Circuit, held at the Thurgood Marshall United States Courthouse, 40 Foley Square, in the City of New York, on the 19th day of June, two thousand fourteen,

Present:

> Reena Raggi,
> Gerard E. Lynch,
> Denny Chin,
> > *Circuit Judges.*

American Atheists, Inc. Dennis Horvitz,
Kenneth Bronstein, Jane Everhart,

> Plaintiffs-Appellants,

ORDER
Docket No. 13-1668

Mark Panzarino,

> Plaintiff,

v.

Port Authority of New York and New Jersey,
World Trade Center Memorial Foundation/
National September 11 Memorial and Museam,

> Defendants-Appellees,

State of New Jersey, Governor Chris Christie,
Silverstein Properties, Inc., Lower Manhattan
Development Corporation, Church of the Holy
Name of Jesus, Brian Jordan, World Trade Center
Properties, LLC,

> Defendants.

Amicus curiae The Becket Fund having challenged plaintiffs' standing in this case, the parties are directed to file on or before July 14, 2014, supplemental briefs of no more than 15 double-spaced pages on the issue of standing.

Plaintiffs' brief should, at a minimum, clarify both the injuries alleged and legal theories relied on to support standing.

Further, to the extent plaintiffs allege that they have been "injured in consequence of having[] a religious tradition that is not their own imposed upon them through the power of the state," First Am. Compl. ¶ 5, because individual plaintiffs view use of the challenged "cross, a Christian symbol, to represent all victims of the 9/11 Attacks" as "offensive," "repugnant," and "insult[ing]" to them as atheists, see id. ¶¶ 6-7, plaintiffs should explain how such offense states a cognizable constitutional injury in light of Town of Greece v. Galloway, 134 S. Ct. 1811, 1815, 1826 (2014) (stating that "[o]ffense . . . does not equate to coercion" merely because government body exposes persons to prayer "they would rather not hear and in which they need not participate"); see also id. at 1826 (citing approvingly to Elk Grove Unified Sch. Dist. v. Newdow, 542 U.S. 1, 44 (2004) (O'Connor, J., concurring) ("[T]he Constitution does not guarantee citizens a right entirely to avoid ideas with which they disagree."); cf. Cooper v. U.S. Postal Serv., 577 F.3d 479, 489-91 (2d Cir. 2009) (recognizing standing where plaintiff was offended by direct contact with religious displays at postal facility nearest his home and was advised to alter his behavior); Sullivan v. Syracuse Hous. Auth., 962 F.2d 1101, 1106-10 (2d Cir. 1992) (recognizing standing where plaintiff was offended by religious after-school program in community center of public housing development in which he lived).

To the extent plaintiffs allege that the challenged cross display "marginalizes them as American citizens," First Am. Compl. ¶ 6, they should explain how this states a particular and concrete injury to them rather than an abstract stigmatization of atheists generally. See United States v. Hays, 515 U.S. 737, 745-46 (1995); Mehdi v. U.S. Postal Serv., 988 F. Supp. 721, 731 (S.D.N.Y. 1997) (Sotomayor, J.).

To the extent plaintiffs reference the Memorial and Museum's receipt of government funding and their own status as taxpayers, see First Am. Compl. ¶¶ 4-5, 32-33, to invoke standing under Flast v. Cohen, 392 U.S. 83 (1968), they should clarify (a) the source of the alleged funding, i.e., federal, state, or local; and (b) whether funds were transmitted pursuant to taxing and spending authority. Plaintiffs should then explain how they satisfy the "logical link" and "nexus" requirements of Flast, see Arizona Christian Sch. Tuition Org. v. Winn, 131 S. Ct. 1436, 1445 (2011), particularly if the funds were "unrestricted," First Am. Compl. ¶¶ 32-33.

Catherine O'Hagan Wolfe
Clerk of Court

Matt explained to me that if the American Atheists Association could successfully prove they had standing in this lawsuit regarding injury then the judges would issue a decision based on the merits of the case. If the American Atheists Association could not prove their legal standing then the three judge panel had the option of throwing the case out altogether since these plaintiffs (the American Atheists) failed to prove their legal interest in the case. This could be extremely embarrassing for the American Atheists Association if their case was to be dismissed. Not only would it prove that this was a classic type of flippant case but this would strengthen Megan Brown's contention that frivolous lawsuits in the future should be penalized. In addition this failed lawsuit would have a fallout effect with serious implications for future lawsuits by other atheist groups. For these future lawsuits there would need to be relevant and valid proof regarding their standing or they run the risk of being jokers like "the boy who cried wolf." This was the exact prediction that the brilliant writer Susan Jacoby had made for this lawsuit in her blog post from early August 2011. On the other hand if there was a decision issued on standing and not on merits then it would be possible for another group of atheists to file another lawsuit and these shenanigans would start all over again. I groaned at the thought of that even happening. "Enough is enough," I lamented to Matt and my fellow friars.

The lawyers for the American Atheists Association and the Museum filed their briefs to argue for standing on July 14, 2014. Wisely the lawyers for the National 9/11 Memorial Museum stated that they supported the concept of standing for the American Atheists Association. They requested that the three judge panel for this appeals case issue a decision based on merits and not on standing! This would mean that if the three judge panel issued a decision based on the merits of the case and ruled in favor of the Museum then not only would the Ground Zero Cross stay in the Museum but the American Atheists Association would officially lose a second time in federal court. There would be little to no chance that the Supreme Court or any other court would hear this case again. Matt and I both wanted the case to be decided on merits. If the three judges decide the appeals case based on merits, then it will be officially over. We were considering filing a paper with the court to urge the judges to decide the issue on the merits but the judges beat us to the punch.

THE THREE WISE JUDGES RULE IN FAVOR OF THE GROUND ZERO CROSS

By mid-July 2014, I was beginning to feel slightly discouraged about the possible outcome of the decision by the court of appeals. If the court ruled that the American Atheists' Association had no standing in this case then there would be no guarantee that another group of atheists' would not file another lawsuit against the Cross in the National 9/11 Memorial Museum. I am not sure if I could take any more legal battles in federal court. As the unofficial guardian of the Ground Zero Cross, I will never give up fighting for this precious relic. Father Mychal Judge, O.F.M., together with 2,982 people did not die in vain. My fellow friars, such as Father John Felice, O.F.M, then the provincial of Holy Name Province, always gave me unswerving support for my ministry at Ground Zero. My own family, especially my parents, faithfully provided me with an abundance of inner strength.

However, when a couple of lawyers told me that this decision might take place in the fall 2014 I began to despair. Why would they take so long? The three judges heard the oral arguments on March 6, 2014. Why would they need more than six months to issue such a key decision? Matt was confident that the three judge panel would rule earlier. I said I hoped so. This is akin to mile 25 of a 26.2 mile marathon – we were so near, yet so far! *Come on already*, I proclaimed to myself in painful frustration. As an inveterate New Yorker, I wanted everything to be better right away and my feelings of frustration were an indicator of that inherent nature. As a Franciscan though I needed to have more patience and understanding. And, really, that is so much easier said than done! How many other Franciscans were sued and taken to Federal court?

ANOTHER EPIPHANY

From July 17-27, 2014, I covered a parish for two weekends in the Bayamon section of the Archdiocese of San Juan, Puerto Rico. I did so as a favor to my fellow Franciscan friar, Archbishop Roberto Octavio Gonzalez, O.F.M. One of his pastors needed a much deserved vacation so I was willing to take up the necessary role. Roberto and I served together in a tough parish in the Southeast Bronx in the 1980's. We both knew our strengths and weaknesses. At the same time, we were both sources of support for one another. Both of our mothers died within a year of one another. As a result, we exchanged messages of consolation and hope given our shared loss.

On Friday, July 25th, 2014, Roberto invited me to lunch to help celebrate my 59th birthday. We dined at a restaurant near his residence in Old San Juan. It was also the Feast of St. James the Apostle, who is the patron saint of Spain as well as of the relatively new diocese of Fajardo-Humacao in Puerto Rico. Roberto shared with me a difficult period of time he experienced in the past two years. He stated that he had trusted in the Lord and prayed that wisdom and common sense would prevail. And he found that it did. He was able to get through his prolonged nightmare. He said that he is now a humbler servant of the Lord and feels so much better.

Although my spiritual dilemma was nothing compared to his resolved "Dark Night of the Soul[7]," I shared with him my present frustration with the appeals case. Roberto took me by the arm and said, "Listen my brother. St. Francis of Assisi never said this would be an easy life. It has its challenges and blessings. Believe me, I should know. I already went through a crisis. But you know what? I made it through. How? I trusted in the Lord and He has made me his instrument of peace and of service to God's people. So Brian, on your birthday, continue to trust in the Lord and be His instrument!" Those words deeply resonated within me, especially when he gave me a birthday gift of a simple rosary he had brought back from Rome. He gave me a warm, fraternal embrace and wished me well on my journey with the Ground Zero Cross. Three years ago I was sued on my birthday and I was very angry. Now three years later I feel much better after conferring with Roberto. He went through a crisis and the Lord pulled him through. Maybe I should heed Roberto's words and do the same, putting all my trust in the Lord.

Two days later on Sunday, July 27th, I returned on the late evening flight from San Juan, Puerto Rico, to New York's JFK airport. During the flight, I was praying the rosary that Roberto gave me for my birthday. I prayed to Our Lady of the Rosary to heal the despair and frustration within me. I prayed that I wanted to trust in the Lord and that He will be the one to guide me in this difficult and trying time. Then, it dawned on me – I am praying in public on an airplane! I felt it was appropriate, and then thought of the three airplanes that were hijacked on the morning of September 11, 2001. I wondered how many people were praying the rosary or praying to God for guidance before those two planes hit the Twin Towers and the other plane crashed near Shanksville, Pennsylvania. I undoubtedly believe that they were terrified for their lives but their trust in the Lord was unshaken regardless.

---

7   "Dark Night of the Soul" – a phrase that comes from St. John of the Cross. As one Franciscan teaches, either you transmit that "dark soul" for the worse, or transform it for the better.

FINISH LINE AND VICTORY – July 28th, 2014

On the morning of July 28th, my prayers were answered so quickly! Thank the Lord and thank Our Lady of the Rosary! All my life, I have heard from my parents, my extended family, my neighbors, my fellow friars and from the Roman Catholic Church to pray and trust in the Lord. Their words were not given to me in vain. I appreciate them all so dearly, and the Lord has blessed me even more than I could ever have imagined.

At about 10:15 AM, I stopped by St. Francis of Assisi Parish in Manhattan where I formerly lived and served. I paid an unexpected visit to fellow friar, David Convertino, O.F.M, and told him I had lunch with his ordination classmate, Archbishop Roberto Gonzalez, O.F.M, on my birthday during a recent visit to Puerto Rico. Lo and behold, at 10:28 AM, I received a text message from my attorney Matt. The message read, "Victory! The court just issued its opinion." I knew exactly what it was without even speaking to Matt. We won the appeals case on its merits. I called Matt right away and he confirmed that the three wise judges ruled on the *merits* of the case and not on the standing issue.

What really made me believe that the Lord was acting in this message was that Matt's message came to me at 10:28 AM. At 10:28 AM on September 11, 2001, the second Tower crashed at the World Trade Center. Every Sunday morning during the recovery operation at Ground Zero, I began Mass near 10:28 AM. This was one of the best messages I have received since Good Friday 2013, when Matt informed me by text that Judge Batts of the Federal District Court ruled in favor of the Ground Zero Cross.

I jumped up in a loud voice and yelled, "HALLELUJAH!" I embraced my fraternal brother David Convertino. As a good fraternal brother, David invited me for prayers and dinner later that evening in the friary of St. Francis of Assisi. After prayers we ate and drank well during dinner. We were celebrating not just a victory for one of the members of the Franciscan fraternity bit a victory for the Ground Zero Cross that had consoled millions of people. While at that dinner I recalled a similar celebration after the Good Friday service on March 29, 2013, at Our Lady of Peace Parish in Brooklyn, N.Y. The friars of the Immaculate Conception Province and I ate and drank well then in celebration of Judge Batts' decision in favor of the Ground Zero Cross that was handed down on Good Friday around 3 PM – the time we believed Jesus Christ died on the Cross. It is interesting to note the Eucharistic symbolism on the two occasions when the Federal District Court and the Second Circuit Federal Court of Appeals handed down their decisions. I was with my Franciscan friars and we celebrated with prayer, good food, and good wine as Jesus did with his disciples at the Last Supper. The Eucharist is the source and summit of our faith as the Second Vatican Council teaches. How great it was to celebrate with my fraternal brothers both these timely decisions!

DECISIONS, DECISIONS, DECISIONS

The July 28th, 44-page decision by the three judge panel was both unanimous and masterfully written. Judge Reena Raggi authored the opinion which was joined in full by the two other judges, Judge Gerald Lynch and Judge Denny Chin. At the outset, they skillfully explain in a short paragraph the background facts of the appeal of the American Atheists:

Specifically, American Atheists contend that the Port Authority and the Foundation (9/11 Memorial Museum) impermissibly promote Christianity in violation of the Establishment Clause and deny atheists equal protection of the laws by displaying the Cross at Ground Zero in the Museum unaccompanied by some item acknowledging that atheists were among the victims and rescuers on September 11. American Atheists acknowledge that there is no historic artifact that speaks particularly to the loss of atheists' lives or to atheists' rescue efforts. Nevertheless they submit that the district court erred in concluding that their claims failed as a matter of law because they are willing to finance an atheists' recognition plaque for display in the Museum together with the Cross at Ground Zero. (p. 6)

For myself and many others in the courtroom on March 6, 2014, the atheists' argument did not make sense at all. At first, they absolutely did not want the Cross in the Museum. Now, they've reversed this train of thought saying it is "permissible" to keep the Cross in the Museum provided that a "memorial plaque" remembering atheists be included in the Museum. The problem with this is that the 9/11 Memorial Museum is *specifically* a memorial museum. You can only include artifacts discovered directly on the site of the tragedy. One cannot simply manufacture a plaque and demand that it be included as an artifact when in truth it is not.

On page 7, the court's reasonable and decisive ruling was proclaimed in clear, succinct words: "For the reasons stated herein, we conclude that the American Atheists' challenge fails on the merits. Accordingly, we hereby affirm the judgment in favor of the appellees." The appellees, in this instance, are the 9/11 Memorial Museum and the Port Authority of New York and New Jersey.

In order to clear up any potential ambiguity, the judges supplied coherent, intelligent reasons for their decision on pages 40 and 41. The bottom paragraph of page 40 reads:

Thus, we conclude that the Equal Protection Clause does not bar appellees from displaying the Cross at Ground Zero in the National September 11 Museum nor does it require them to supplement the museum's "Finding Meaning" exhibition with an atheist recognition plaque as appellants propose.

The Conclusion (pp. 41-42) was so well-written and definitive that many lawyers including my classmate John Coughlin, O.F.M, and Matt Dowd believe it is highly unlikely that the U.S. Supreme Court would take this case since the three judges unanimously upheld Judge Batts March 29, 2013 Federal District court decision.

III. **Conclusion**

To summarize, we conclude as follows:

1. Displaying the Cross at Ground Zero in the National September 11 Museum does not violate the Establishment Clause because:
    a. the stated purpose of displaying The Cross at Ground Zero is to tell the story of how some people used faith to cope with the tragedy is genuine and an objective observer would understand the purpose of the display to be secular;
    b. an objective observer would not view the display as endorsing religion generally or Christianity specifically because it is part of an exhibit entitled "Finding Meaning at Ground Zero." The exhibit includes various nonreligious as well as religious artifacts that people at Ground Zero used for solace and the textual displays accompanying the cross communicate its historical significance within this larger context; and
    c. c. there is no evidence that the static display of this genuine historic artifact excessively entangles the government with religion.

2. In the absence of any Establishment Clause violation or any evidence of discriminatory animus towards atheists, the Museum did not deny equal protection by displaying The Cross at Ground Zero and refusing plaintiffs' request to fund an accompanying symbol commemorating atheists.

Accordingly, the district court's award of summary judgment is AFFIRMED.

UNITED STATES COURT OF APPEALS

FOR THE SECOND CIRCUIT

_____

August Term, 2013

(Argued: March 6, 2014   Decided: July 28, 2014)

Docket No. 13-1668-cv

_____

AMERICAN ATHEISTS, INC., DENNIS HORVITZ, KENNETH BRONSTEIN,
JANE EVERHART,

Plaintiffs-Appellants,

MARK PANZARINO,

Plaintiff,

— v. —

PORT AUTHORITY OF NEW YORK AND NEW JERSEY, NATIONAL SEPTEMBER 11
MEMORIAL AND MUSEUM AT THE WORLD TRADE CENTER FOUNDATION, INC.,

Defendants-Appellees,

1

III.   Conclusion

To summarize, we conclude as follows:

1.   Displaying The Cross at Ground Zero in the National September 11 Museum does not violate the Establishment Clause because:

a.   the stated purpose of displaying The Cross at Ground Zero to tell the story of how some people used faith to cope with the tragedy is genuine, and an objective observer would understand the purpose of the display to be secular;

b.   an objective observer would not view the display as endorsing religion generally, or Christianity specifically, because it is part of an exhibit entitled "Finding Meaning at Ground Zero"; the exhibit includes various nonreligious as well as religious artifacts that people at Ground Zero used for solace; and the textual displays accompanying the cross communicate its historical significance within this larger context; and

c.   there is no evidence that the static display of this genuine historic artifact excessively entangles the government with religion.

2.   In the absence of any Establishment Clause violation or any evidence of discriminatory animus toward atheists, the Museum did not deny

41

equal protection by displaying The Cross at Ground Zero and refusing plaintiffs' request to fund an accompanying symbol commemorating atheists.

Accordingly, the district court's award of summary judgment is AFFIRMED.

What I find truly fascinating is that the essential elements of the court's decisions echoed the primary points in the *amicus brief* Matt sent to the Second Circuit on my behalf in November 2013. The matters of the Establishment Clause, the Equal Protection Clause and my right to bless objects in public were all addressed in both the *amicus brief* and in the final, unanimous decision of the Second Circuit.

After ten years of fighting with various government agencies and three years of fighting the American Atheists Association in the Federal Court system passionate and courageous believers got to see their vision finally fulfilled. These were the ones who signed a petition in favor of the Ground Zero Cross, over 300,000 of them, including Gary LaBarbera, Ed Malloy, Richard Sheirer, and Jane Pollicino, who collected 5,000 signatures herself. They must certainly feel spiritually AFFIRMED after all of their hard work and mine as well. Pope Francis couldn't have put it any better with a statement he gave during his visit to the 9/11 Memorial on September 25th, 2015: "This place of death became a place of life too, a place of sacred lives, a hymn to the triumph of life over the prophets of destruction and death, to goodness over evil, to reconciliation and unity over hatred and division" (Origins 332).

may not have been lost in vain.

Comfort and console us, strengthen
us in hope,
and give us the wisdom and courage
to work tirelessly for a world
where true peace and love reign
among nations and in the hearts of all.

* * *

Speech

I feel many different emotions standing
here at ground zero, where thousands
of lives were taken in a senseless act
of destruction. Here grief is palpable.
The water we see flowing toward that
empty pit reminds us of all those lives
that fell prey to those who think that
destruction, tearing down, is the only
way to settle conflicts. It is the silent cry
of those who were victims of a mindset
that knows only violence, hatred and
revenge. A mindset that can only cause
pain, suffering, destruction and tears.

*"This place of death became
a place of life too, a place of
saved lives, a hymn to the triumph of life over the prophets of destruction and death,
to goodness over evil, to reconciliation and unity over
hatred and division."*

The flowing water is also a symbol
of our tears. Tears at so much devastation and ruin, past and present. This is
a place where we shed tears, we weep
out of a sense of helplessness in the face
of injustice, murder and the failure to
settle conflicts through dialogue. Here
we mourn the wrongful and senseless
loss of innocent lives because of the
inability to find solutions that respect
the common good. This flowing water
reminds us of yesterday's tears but also
of all the tears still being shed today.

A few moments ago I met some of
the families of the fallen first responders. Meeting them made me see once
again how acts of destruction are never
impersonal, abstract or merely material. They always have a face, a concrete
story, names. In those family members
we see the face of pain, a pain that still
touches us and cries out to heaven.

At the same time, those family members showed me the other face of this
attack, the other face of their grief:
the power of love and remembrance.
A remembrance that does not leave us
empty and withdrawn. The name of so
many loved ones are written around the
towers' footprints. We can see them, we
can touch them and we can never forget
them.

Here, amid pain and grief, we also
have a palpable sense of the heroic
goodness people are capable of, those
hidden reserves of strength from
which we can draw. In the depths of
pain and suffering you also witnessed
the heights of generosity and service.
Hands reached out, lives were given. In
a metropolis that might seem impersonal, faceless, lonely, you demon-
strated the powerful solidarity born of
mutual support, love and self-sacrifice.
No one thought about race, nationality,
neighborhoods, religion or politics. It
was all about solidarity, meeting immediate needs, brotherhood. It was about
being brothers and sisters. New York
City firemen walked into the crumbling
towers with no concern for their own
well-being. Many succumbed; their
sacrifice enabled great numbers to be
saved.

This place of death became a place
of life too, a place of saved lives, a hymn
to the triumph of life over the prophets
of destruction and death, to goodness
over evil, to reconciliation and unity
over hatred and division.

In this place of sorrow and remembrance I am filled with hope as I have
the opportunity to join with leaders
representing the many religious traditions that enrich the life of this great
city. I trust that our presence together
will be a powerful sign of our shared
desire to be a force for reconciliation,
peace and justice in this community
and throughout the world.

For all our differences and disagreements, we can experience a world of
peace. In opposing every attempt to
create a rigid uniformity, we can and
must build unity on the basis of our
diversity of languages, cultures and religions, and lift our voices against everything that would stand in the way of
such unity. Together we are called to
say no to every attempt to impose uniformity and yes to a diversity accepted
and reconciled.

This can only happen if we uproot
from our hearts all feelings of hatred,
vengeance and resentment. We know
that that is only possible as a gift from
heaven. Here, in this place of remembrance, I would ask everyone together,
each in his or her own way, to spend a
moment in silence and prayer. Let us
implore from on high the gift of commitment to the cause of peace. Peace
in our homes, our families, our schools
and our communities. Peace in all those
places where war never seems to end.
Peace for those faces which have known
nothing but pain. Peace throughout this
world God has given us as the home of
all and a home for all. Simply PEACE.
Let us pray in silence.

(Moment of silence.)

In this way the lives of our dear ones
will not be lives that will one day be
forgotten. Instead, they will be present whenever we strive to be prophets
not of tearing down but of building up,
prophets of reconciliation, prophets of
peace. ∎

U.S. Visit: Visit to
School in Harlem

Pope Francis

*Pope Francis encouraged an audience
of New York Catholic school students
and immigrants to live with joy and
dare to dream. He also highlighted the
immigrant experience — in a way children could understand, comparing it to
seeking acceptance and making friends
in school, not always an easy place for
them to fit in or find their way. "They
tell me that one of the nice things about
this school ... is that some students come
from other places and many from other
countries," Pope Francis told students
and a group of immigrants at the Our
Lady Queen of Angels School in Harlem,
where he visited Sept. 25. "I know that
it is not easy to have to move and find a
new home, to meet new neighbors and
new friends," the pope said. "As the beginning it can be pretty hard. ... Often you
have to learn a new language, adjust to a
new culture. ... There is so much to learn!
And not just homework." The message
continued the pope's call for inclusive*

CHAPTER 5

The Way Of The Cross

"My wish is that all of us… will have the courage to walk in the presence of the Lord, with the Lord's Cross; to build the Church on the Lord's blood which was poured out on the Cross… and in this way, the Church will go forward."

– Pope Francis, *Homily from the Missa Pro Ecclesia*, March 2013.

The Way of the Cross is not just something exclusively observed during the season of Lent. It is a daily journey of faith that requires patience, perseverance, and prayer. I have been commemorating the Way of the Ground Zero Cross since September 23, 2001. Throughout my journey with the Cross I have indeed persevered, and prayed but I admit I was not always a "shining beacon of patience" in those years. Nonetheless I am wholeheartedly devoted to the Ground Zero Cross till the day I die. Why, you ask? Well, I sincerely believe that the Cross has given meaning for those searching for answers about why 9/11 even occurred. In the early stages of post-9/11, I saw the blood on the ground, the blood on bodies and body parts, and even people donating blood for a worthy cause. I saw bodies. I saw burnt flesh. I saw countless body parts all over that sacred ground. I never saw the blood of Jesus on the Cross at Calvary but I did see the blood of many who either believed or did not believe in Jesus Christ. On 9/11 I saw the blood of the People of God and how they perished as victims. Since September 23, 2001 I saw Christ the Victor in the faces of those who gazed on the Ground Zero Cross in which they had found hope. New York City is renowned for its multicultural, multilingual and multi-complicated brand of people and lifestyle. I love it. The Roman Catholic Church has always emphasized cultural pluralism which includes respect for all races, colors and creeds. Our faith is one among many faiths not only in this city but also in our nation and around the world. All those who believe in God are protected by the First Amendment. The reverse is, of course, true as well – those who do not believe in God, like my doctor, are also protected by the First Amendment. I cannot proselytize[8] any faith among the atheists and agnostics. At the same time, others cannot take away my First Amendment right to bless an object in public and make an interpretation of what I think is sacred. Remember from the first chapter that this Ground Zero Cross was actually built as a T-beam to support a frame of a government building. It was *never* meant to be a Cross. However due to the events of 9/11 many faith-filled people interpreted it as a Cross. It was a free-flowing, collective interpretation. Before attempts are made to move the Ground Zero Cross out of sight may I suggest that every telephone pole in New York City be removed? They look like Crosses to me! An interpretation is simply that – an interpretation. All are entitled to this. Since when do we start making incendiary judgments against interpretations? If that is the case, then start closing down all museums and art galleries!

THE FUTURE OF THE GROUND ZERO CROSS

In mid-May 2014, the National 9/11 Memorial Museum finally opened after years of political football, fundraising problems, construction cost overruns and whatever else I am not aware of and lies hidden. I am truly happy for the Museum especially Alice Greenwald and her dedicated staff. I understand that they have done a great job. I heard from many who have visited that it is a magnificent museum. As for my concerns, many friends and colleagues confirmed what I thought would happen. The Ground Zero Cross is present but is not in as prominent a place as it should be. There could be a variety of factors to explain this lack of prominence. I suspect that the lawsuit by the American Atheists Association influenced the decision for a less conspicuous place. In addition, as I have mentioned, the National 9/11 Memorial Museum refused my continued requests in 2010 to guarantee in writing that it would receive a prominent place. Therefore

---

8   Proselytize – convert or attempt to convert (someone) from one religion, belief, or opinion to another.

I am neither surprised nor angry that it is not in a more proper location. I have no control over that decision. However I am consoled by Mychal Judge's memorable prayer: "Lord, take me where you want me to go; let me meet who you want me to meet; tell me what You want me to say; and keep me out of your way." The fact remains that the Ground Zero Cross will always have a community of support inside and outside the museum.

While I reflect upon the meaning of this iconic Cross there are many other significant people who figuratively carried the Cross besides the underrated union construction workers who lost 61 workers on 9/11. Some of these individuals were the ones who devoted themselves to the events and effects of 9/11. They are FDNY Chief Joseph Pfeifer whose company was the first to respond to the attack on the Twin Towers. Among his fellow 343 firefighters who died that day was his own brother, Lt. Kevin Pfeifer, FDNY. Chief Pfeifer and I both prayed for his brother on the National Day of Prayer on September 14, 2001. Minutes later we shook hands and personally prayed with President George W. Bush at Ground Zero. Quite poignant. NYPD Chief Joseph Esposito was another. He lost 23 police officers on that fateful day. His faith and professional experience were evident when he evenly challenged and consoled the police department during the entire recovery period. "Espo" was one of the few who attended every Midnight Mass I celebrated at Ground Zero from Christmas Eve 2001 to Christmas Eve 2012. There was Lt. John Ryan, PAPD, who lost 37 members of the Port Authority Police Department and Ken Ringler former chairman of the Port Authority New York-New Jersey. Both men genuinely cared for the families of the victims of 9/11 both police and civilian. It was Sal Annerino, Andrew Macchio and the "Strongest" of the NYC Department of Sanitation who did the masterful job of the cleanup work that took place during the recovery period – efforts that still go unrecognized in the many media accounts of 9/11. They attended every Mass at the Cross at Ground Zero.

There were also those people who participated in the recovery period who truly didn't have to but chose to do so out of the goodness of their hearts. The Salvation Army and countless volunteers offered their time, talent and treasure to console not only the recovery workers but particularly family members and friends of the victims. They escorted many to the Masses by the Cross for a sign of comfort and consolation. There were others like Anna Ivotsa of Russia and Ken Allen of Australia. In a microcosm, they represent the international tragedy of 9/11. Besides the United States it is estimated that 80 other nations lost loved ones. Anna lost her husband in Tower One. He worked for a foreign financial firm. Anna is Russian Orthodox and found great comfort in the Ground Zero Cross.

She has returned to Siberia, Russia, to help underprivileged families. Ken was the Consul General of Australia to New York City at the time of the attack. He was responsible for sending the bodies of 12 Australians back to their home country. He was also called to offer support and comfort for the victims' families and fellow Australians in the New York area. A self-described struggling Protestant he and his family sought comfort in the Cross as well. Ken has returned to Australia and is part of the solution regarding multicultural and multilingual issues.

LESSONS LEARNED

Upon reflection, overall, I have gained so much along my journey with the Ground Zero Cross. As the first chapter progressed I gained knowledge about architecture and design from new-found friends in the construction industry. My theological education taught me that the symbol of the cross precedes Christianity. It was only appropriated by Christians since the Cross made Jesus Christ a victim by execution. Nevertheless the Resurrection of Jesus made him a Victor over death. As such, the promise of eternal life is for all who believe and worship. A community of support comes for all who share tragedy and pain whether we believe in God or not. "We have seen evil at its worst, but goodness at its best." This was the basis for the first chapter. The second chapter was the living continuation of the Way of the Cross or in this case the Way of the Ground Zero Cross. It was a path that demanded much – patience, perseverance, prayer, and street smarts, courtesy of Ed Malloy and Gary LaBarbera The third chapter and fourth chapters are meant to emphasize the need to protect religious liberty for all who believe in God. At the same time it serves to teach us to be sensitive and understanding of those who do not believe in God. An added precaution regarding legal matters is to enlist legal assistance for individuals and institutions who may become targets of lawsuits by those who may not fully comprehend that religious liberty is protected by the First Amendment. The role of the laity is very important as the majority of the clergy, and other religious figures like myself who are not acquainted with civil law will need help from people like Matt Dowd and organizations that seek to protect religious liberty in the public square. Beware of the threat of future lawsuits! Finally at the end of this long and winding road in this fifth chapter, I am "better not bitter." Really, I am *better* for this prolonged Way of the Cross. As a native New Yorker and Franciscan I wish the American Atheists Association and the National 9/11 Memorial Museum well in their future endeavors. My mother and father always taught me to abide by integrity and honesty and to pursue the common good. During this particular Way of the Cross the common thread linking all of these noble traits was woven through the union construction workers led by Ed Malloy and dedicated public servants like Richard Sheirer who worked for NYPD, FDNY and OEM. May they both rest in peace. May we all have peace on earth and good will to all. As the Holy Father, Pope Francis says, "let us go forward!"

CHAPTER 6

ORIGIN AND HISTORY OF THE CROSS AT THE WORLD TRADE CENTER

> "Knowledge is like a garden. If it is not cultivated, it cannot be harvested."
>
> – A Guinean Saying.

The purpose of this part is to prove that the historical artifact known as the Cross at Ground Zero was originally built as a cruciform structure. It was not welded together artificially after 9/11 to resemble a Cross. It was built as a Cross-like beam! This cross-like beam, like many others, was a part of the construction inserted into World Trade Center 6 and in place when it officially opened in 1973. This part will also provide a brief history of the concept of the Cross.

BACKGROUND OF THE CRUICIFORM STRUCTURE

The concept of the World Trade Center was officially launched by David Rockefeller in the 1950's. According to the Port Authority of New York and New Jersey the objective of the World Trade Center was to centralize in one location a vast number of critically important services and functions relating to the foreign trade of the ports of New York and New Jersey. Lower Manhattan has served as the original anchor for the settlement of New York City and continues to be the perpetual symbolic frontier for expected immigrants and global financial powers alike. With the birth of the idea in 1946 for a large office development on the lower Hudson, a World Trade Center, New York City was once again launching ahead with a remaking of itself (Fernandez 5).

World Trade Center Towers 1 and 2 had been designed to produce a large-scale global audience. It is likely that over 2 million people a year came from all over the world to stand at the top of the Towers and to see what the Towers themselves "saw". Both Towers evoked a magnificent panorama in New York Harbor with both New York State and New Jersey serving as admirable vistas. The design architect chosen for this massive task was the Japanese American, Minoru Yamasaki of Yamasaki and Associates. Leslie Robertson was the project's lead structural engineer, and as such was the person who led the team of designers responsible for specifying the details that resulted in the steel assemblies in World Trade Center 6 resembling crosses. Leslie E. Robertson Associates (LERA), the firm bearing his name, continues to operate today.

Proof of my claim that the Ground Zero Cross was built like a cross, but never intended to be a Christian sacred object, came from the head engineer of LERA, Dan Sesil, who informed me at a luncheon meeting that "during the construction of World Trade Center 6, segments of steel beams were shop attached to columns thereby creating assemblies that were used in various places in the project. Therefore, we were able to determine its exact location in the original construction." The Ground Zero Cross was never intended to be a cross, but we, the recovery workers and family members of 9/11 victims, interpreted it to be a cross. Are not interpretations protected under the First Amendment?

The World Trade Center buildings also provided extraordinary employment opportunities for the construction workers of the region. More than 3,500 people were employed continuously on-site during construction. A total of 10,000 people were involved in its construction. Tragically, 60 workers were killed during construction (Fernandez 9). As the chaplain for the union construction workers of New York City, I find that number to be of solemn interest. 60 workers were killed on-site during the construction of the Towers from 1967 to 1972. In comparison, 61 union workers were killed within two hours on 9/11. According to Willie Quinlan, a retired ironworker of Local 40 of the International Ironworkers of North America, both Tower 1 and Tower 2 began construction in 1967. Willie was an apprentice at the time and was present when both Towers were completed in 1973. Willie was also aware that other World Trade Center buildings were going up after he completed his tasks on World Trade Center 1 and 2 in 1973. World Trade Center 6 was designed to be an eight story building, having the fewest floors of any building within the World Trade Center site. World Trade Center 6 measured 537,693 square feet. It stood 92 feet (28 meters), but was actually 105 feet (32 meters) above ground. According to Port Authority records, the steel from World Trade Center 6 was provided from Stevens/ Harris Steel Company which was based in Carlstadt, New Jersey, in the late 1960's.

Who were the tenants of World Trade Center 6 on the morning of 9/11? According to records, the tenants of that building were the New York City offices of the U.S. Customs Service, the U.S. Department of Commerce, the U.S. Bureau of Alcohol, Tobacco and Firearms, U.S. Department of Agriculture, Administrator of the Animals and Plant Health Inspection Services (AAPHIS), U.S. Department of Labor, and the Peace Corps and the Export-Import Bank of the U.S. Eastco Building. After the discovery of the Cross at Ground Zero, I immediately noted the irony that the iconic Cross came from a building that housed primarily U.S. government agencies. There were so many other ironies and contradictions that took place in the aftermath of 9/11.

In an insightful book about the architectural significance of the World Trade Center buildings after the tragedy of 9/11, Mark Wigley wrote, "Buildings are meant to last longer than people. Shelter is as much emotional as it is physical. Architects craft time when they craft space. People are really grieving for themselves when they grieve for buildings" (Wigley 71). Why did this tragedy happen? Many conjecture that the key, symbolic role of the World Trade Center, the rationale behind its design and its destruction, was to represent the global marketplace. This might explain why those responsible for the terrorist attack chose these particular buildings when they devised such a diabolical strategy.

I am grateful that new buildings and a sense of social cohesion have taken hold in place of that terrible tragedy. Many believe as do I that the new buildings have done much to heal both the physical and psychological wounds left in the wake of such a traumatic event. By way of illustration it is no coincidence that the new One World Trade Center stands at the site where the World Trade Center once stood. The very place where the Ground Zero Cross was discovered in the rubble of World Trade Center 6 is now the site of the tallest building in the United States – a beacon of hope for all who may need it.

CHAPTER 7

THE GROUND ZERO CROSS: ORIGINS OF FAITH

> "God proved His love on the Cross. When Christ hung and bled and died, it was God saying to the world, 'I love you!'"
>
> — Reverend Billy Graham.

The Cross has had significance centuries before the founding of Christianity. I have often been told by many wise people never to presume other people know what you are talking about. I am not going to presume that most people know about the origin of the Cross. The symbol of the Cross long preceded Christianity. It has been found painted on cave walls as an expression of some kind. Eventually it became a cruel means of torture and execution. The Ground Zero Cross was founded at a place of execution but was seen as a sign of inspiration and meaning to all who gazed on it.

One scholar asserts, "The Cross is the oldest symbol in the world. Centuries before the Christian era ancient crosses were in use as pagan emblems. They have been found carved in stone dating back to remote ages." (Benson 16). The Cross dates back to great antiquity. It differed in shapes, sizes, and designs as did the ancient peoples and civilizations. It appears that through the ages the cross has existed and had vital significance and influence for a variety of reasons other than just a symbol of faith (Benson 16). Many historians note that the simple equilateral cross was symbolic of space, the earth and sky. It is one of the earliest forms of ancient crosses and was traced on walls and carved in stone long before the birth of Christ (Benson 17).

Herodotus records that the earliest record of crucifixion dates back to the beginning of the Persian period (6th century BC). Later Persian history is replete with stories of crucifixion (Pritchard 389 – incorrect citation, needs update). Interestingly, J. B. Pritchard asserts that the oldest written reference to impalement is contained in the Code of Hammurabi dating from about 1700 B.C. (Pritchard 389 – incorrect citation, needs update).

Proof of my claim that the Cross preceded Christianity is evident in Professor Benson's findings. "Almost from the beginning of recorded history, there was another cross in frequent use known as the Tau Cross. In form it resembled the capital T. It has been called the cross of the Old Testament as it was known to the Jews. They may possibly have become familiar with it during their bondage to the Egyptians as a cross resembling the Tau Cross with a loop at the top appeared frequently in Egyptian hieroglyphs and carved on their ancient sepulchers and monuments" (Benson 20). There are two observations to make about the Jewish-Egyptian influence of the Tau Cross. First, there is scant evidence that the ancient Hebrews used the cross as a means of execution. They usually stoned people to death. However, it appeared that on rare occasions, crucifixion on a cross was used since the time of Abraham. Professor Benson argues that that the famous gallows of Haman was a cross (Benson 20?). On the other hand, my good friend during the recovery period of 9/11 Rabbi Joseph Potasnik, a chaplain to the Fire Department of New York, informed me that "Although I acknowledge that crucifixion preceded Christianity, crucifixion was always something foreign to Jewish law" (Rabbi Potasnik. Personal interview. July 4, 2006).

Second, as a Franciscan friar, the fascinating aspect of this explanation of the Tau Cross is that in the 13th century, St. Francis of Assisi and the early friars appropriated the Tau Cross as a means to express their Franciscan devotion to the Cross. Many Franciscan scholars teach that the origin of the Tau Cross in the Franciscan tradition definitely came from the Old Testament (Armstrong O.F.M.Cap., Regis. Interview by Franciscan scholar. July 10, 1978). Another form of the Cross that preceded Christianity was the Greek Cross that was used by various ancient races. It was simple in design, an upright line crossed at right angles by a horizontal line (Benson 20). The primitive Greek Cross was in use for over a thousand years before the Christian era. Interestingly, it was in the same form as the Modern Greek Christian Cross whose form, except for ornamentation, is unchanged from the ancient Pagan Cross (Benson 21). Later, among the Roman and Latin peoples, another ancient cross was much in use. It resembled the Greek cross, but with a longer vertical beam. At that time, it was called the Latin Cross, but it is now better known as the Christian cross.

Why do I bring these historical resources to light? I would like to establish that the Cross was never solely a Christian symbol throughout world history as some people mistakenly held when the Ground Zero Cross was first discovered. From the three ancient crosses – the Tau, the Greek, and the Latin – have evolved all the varied forms and designs of the Christian Cross (Benson 21).

Allow me to explain the purpose of crucifixion. According to the New Catholic Encyclopedia, "Crucifixion was a method of capital punishment commonly used among the ancient peoples surrounding the Mediterranean basis from approximately the 6th century BC to the 4th century AD. Because of its cruelty, crucifixion was introduced as both a severe punishment of the victim and a frightful deterrent to others (*New Catholic Encyclopedia* 389). According to Roman tradition, the cross was fifteen feet high, but usually crosses used for executions were not more than ten feet. It was part of the disgrace of the condemned that "he should bear his cross to the place of execution" (Benson 25). This was the kind of gallows used by the Romans for the execution of criminals. Since it was considered so shameful a penalty by law no Roman citizen could be crucified. Roman crucifixion was always preceded by a scourging of the victim at the place of judgment (Pritchard 391). Slaves and the condemned of other and despised races were put to death either on a single stake driven through their bodies or they were bound or nailed to a Cross (Benson 24).

Crucifixion was a terrible means of a slow, torturous death. It had a double meaning for the Roman Empire – to punish and humiliate a victim in public while at the same time creating havoc and fear in the victim's surviving community. Visual evidence of this twofold meaning was revealed in the last scene of the movie epic "Spartacus." Spartacus was a Jewish rebel who was trained to fight as a gladiator under Roman rule. When he escaped from Roman power he began a revolt against Roman rule and sought to escape with many other Jews and those under Roman subjugation. Unfortunately he was defeated in battle and arrested again and sentenced to death by crucifixion for his alleged crimes against the Roman Empire. While hanging on the cross-like structure and awaiting certain death he came upon his newly-freed wife and their new born baby. He was consoled not only by their presence but by the realization that they had both found freedom – something Spartacus and his followers always yearned for and desired. When they departed for their new home Spartacus gave a brave smile and knew that he would not die in vain.

I always have that image in mind when I think of the first uniformed responders – among them my mentor, Father Mychal Judge. They all knew that at the very minute they entered the Two Towers there was the possibility they may never return to their loved ones. However those 343 FDNY firefighters, 37 PAPD police officers, and 23 NYPD police officers did not die in vain either. They made sure over 28,000 people returned safely to their loved ones.

CHRISTIAN MEANING OF THE CROSS

The devotion to Jesus Christ dying on a Cross through crucifixion was not immediately embraced as a sign of faith for the first followers of the Messiah. Rather the Roman use of the Cross still applied as a means of instilling fear in the victim's local community. There was no devotion but rather a genuine and understandable fear of the Cross. As Professor Benson writes, "The necessity of caution to escape persecution was also a strong incentive. The caution that led them to conceal themselves and their dead in the catacombs would make them use a less obvious symbol of their faith" (Benson 40). On occasion, some would draw a cross on the walls of the catacombs to illustrate the means of death of their Savior but this was a teaching method done in seclusion from Roman authority.

The first symbol of Christian faith was not the cross. It was actually the fish. In Greek, "ichtos" means fish. Since the majority of the 12 Apostles were fishermen and many people observed the miracles of Jesus from a boat on the water and his use of both agrarian and seafaring imagery the early Christians chose the sign of the fish to identify themselves as Christians and also to avoid detection by the Roman authorities.

The fact is that the Cross was not used by the early Christians as a symbol of their faith and it did not come into general use until three centuries later. Why? Many New Testament scholars teach that the worship of the Cross was not encouraged because of the stern commands that Jesus Christ gave not to worship any idol or graven image. Moreover it was unlikely that an instrument of execution and disgrace would become a focus of sacrifice and redemption (Benson 40). To reiterate, the Ground Zero Cross being discovered in a place of execution is a source of inspiration and comfort for many after the tragedy.

When did the Cross gain prominence in the Christian world? In the early fourth century, the attitude and perspective of the Cross shifted significantly through the efforts of the Roman Emperor Constantine. Jerome Murphy-O'Connor, O.P., a well-known New Testament scholar has made these points:

1. Emperor Constantine was victorious in the Battle of the Milvian Bridge in 312. He saw a luminous Cross in a dream. His victory opened the way to the legalization of Christianity.

2. Out of respect for Christ's death on the Cross, Emperor Constantine forbade crucifixion as a means of execution. It was no longer part of people's experience.

3. A new meaning came about by the discovery of the True Cross during the construction of the Church of the Holy Sepulchre in Jerusalem. It was made of wood and was similar to the Tree of Life.

4. In the last analysis it is due to the letters of St. Paul (not just the 4 gospels) that the Cross, an instrument of torture, became a Christian symbol.

5. The Cross is the place of the ultimate transformation where God is revealed precisely as the powerless One who embraces our powerlessness to the underlying benefit of both (Murphy-O'Connor 21-2).

I vividly recall taking a seminar with Dr. Dreyer. She constantly challenged her audience to "not only pray to the Cross, but make a connection with the Cross and your everyday life." I never forgot that wise admonition. I remember that three days after September 11, 2001, the Feast of the Exaltation of the Cross took place on September 14th. I was then unaware that Frank Silecchia, the Local 731 construction worker, had first encountered the Cross at Ground Zero on the previous day, the 13th. However despite the magnitude of sadness and shock the recovery workers and I made the sign of the Cross in the hopes that prospective survivors would be found and saved. We still had high hopes in those first few days – life on high in Christ Jesus through the Cross. Dreyer teaches:

"In each historical period, Christians turn to the cross for understanding, meaning, encouragement and challenge amid the particular joys and sufferings distinct to each era, geography and situation. Yet in and through these concrete and specific circumstances, we conclude that the meaning of the cross is love." (Murphy-O'Connor 253)

The Cross gives meaning to our lives. The meaning of the Christian cross is clear and significant. It is the symbol of life eternal, of redemption and resurrection through faith. This is why it has been of real, vital significance to millions of believers since the day Christ suffered death on a Cross (Benson 23).

Not only has the Cross found fame through artwork in churches, chapels and museums but it has been part of the local community for a variety of purposes. For example the Cross has been used much as it is today both for commemorative and monumental purposes. Every soldier's or sailor's grave on foreign battlefields, whether Catholic or Protestant, is marked by a Cross, while for Jews it is the Star of David. Many memorial monuments consist of a granite or marble cross with the crusader's sword carved upon its face (Benson 83). Other Crosses posed great importance in public areas. There are memorial Crosses for those who died as a group and Market Crosses to bring the message of God to the busy community that might not always attend services in houses of worship. There were Wayside Crosses in which the wayfarer stopped and prayed on his or her journey (Benson 95).

The Cross is the greatest and most prolific of all Christian imagery. It typifies the Savior and his sacrifice, the symbol of suffering and salvation. It is also designated as the Passion Cross and the Cross of Calvary. As such, it is always set on a base of three steps symbolizing the Trinity and the three Christian virtues of faith, hope, and charity. Furthermore, the four points of the Cross were a symbolic reminder that the redeemed were gathered from the four quarters of the earth (Benson 107).

Considering what has been previously stated what did Jesus Christ really mean by carrying the Cross? "Christ admonished his disciples [saying] that if they would be His followers they must carry the Cross. His command probably had little meaning to them because the cross was a sign of execution and not a sign of faith as we later developed this concept. The apostles did not comprehend that the Cross was symbolic. It was the cross of sacrifice and self-denial they were to hear. Christ proclaimed that it was God's will that all who believed and followed him must endure the cross of sorrow or misfortune patiently and without complaint. Even the loss of health or property or the death of loved ones must be borne without bitterness or complaint" (Benson 188). Thy will be done. For those who lost a loved one from 9/11 and for those who served as recovery workers, doing God's will often meant the loss of personal gain or pleasure. It was a sacrifice for others. This is what it means to bear the cross of Christ.

Since 9/11, I have found great comfort in the Greek Orthodox description of the Cross of Christ. Christ was both a Victim and a Victor. He was Victim of an unfair trail, an unjust persecution, a forced, humiliating procession to Calvary, a slow, deliberate death through crucifixion. Days later, he was Victor of Life over Death and fulfilled the promise of His rise from the dead on the third day. He gave us the promise of everlasting life.

There were many chaplains from different faiths who served at Ground Zero for those nine months. Many blessed the bodies or body parts as I did during that recovery period. Often times when a chaplain was not found to bless the body and body parts, an ecumenical prayer composed by Catholic and Protestant chaplains was read by the recovery workers. It was entitled "A Prayer of Recovery", and it is as follows:

A Prayer of Recovery

"Remember, O Lord, this your servant, who is gone before us with the sign of faith and now sleeps in the sleep of peace. To this one, O Lord and to all who have died at the World Trade Center, grant we pray, a place of refreshment, light and peace. Amen."

Those present concluded the prayer with the sign of the cross. Note the irony of the sign of the cross – the place of execution has become the place for inspiration and comfort through the faith surrounding the Ground Zero Cross.

WORKS CITED

Steinauer, Jennifer. *A Nation Challenged: The Site: A Symbol of Faith Marks a City's Hallowed Ground*. The New York Times. Oct. 5, 2001. B12.

Murphy, Dean E. *A Nation Challenged: Christmas Mass Beneath a Cross of Fallen Steel*. The New York Times. Dec. 26, 2001. A1.

Daly, Michael. *It's Hallowed Ground Zero*. The New York Daily News. March 31, 2002.

Colford, Paul D. *Rev. Standing Guard Over WTC 'cross'*. The New York Daily News. Apr. 13, 2006.

Appleton, Michael. *7f40mkaz.jpg*. The New York Daily News. April 11, 2006.

Konigsberg, Eric. *Brief Journey for an Icon of the Attack on New York*. The New York Times. Oct. 6, 2006.

Jones, Kevin J. Personal interview, Catholic News Agency, July 29, 2011

Jacoby, Susan. blog post "Atheist group's frivolous lawsuit aims to bar "cross" from 9/11 museum." The Washington Post. August 1, 2011.

Excerpt from Editorial on 9/11 cross lawsuit. The Washington Post. August 9, 2011.

L'Osservatore Romano There was an accompanying picture of myself blessing the Cross with Rudy Giuliani, Richard Sheirer, and Frank Silecchia in the background. (pg 15 #32-33, August 10-17, 2011).

Caher, John. Circuit Upholds 9/11 Display of Cross-Shaped Metal Beam. New York Law Journal, July 29, 2014, 1

Pope Francis. U.S. Visit: Interreligious Gathering at 9/11 Memorial. Origins: Catholic News Service, Oct. 8, 2015, vol.45. number 19, 332

Benson, George Willard. *The Cross: Its History and Symbolism*. 1934. Dover Publications, Inc., 2005.

Murphy-O'Connor, Jerome, et al. *The Cross in Christian Tradition: From Paul to Bonaventure*. Edited by Elizabeth Dreyer. Paulist Press. 2000.

Pritchard, James B., editor. *Ancient Near Eastern Texts Relating to the Old Testament with Supplement*. Princeton University Press. 1955.

"Crucifixion", New Catholic Encyclopedia, 2nd. ed. vol.4 389 Thomas Gale: Catholic University of America: Washington DC 2003

Fernandez, John E. "A brief history of the World Trade Center Towers." *The Towers Lost and Beyond: A Collection of essays on the World Trade Center by researchers at the Massachusetts Institute of Technology*, edited by Eduardo Kausel, MIT Press, 2002, 5; 9.

Wigley, Mark. "Insecurity by Design." *After the World Trade Center: Rethinking New York City*, edited by Michael Sorkin and Sharon Zukin, Routledge:Taylor &Francis Group, New York, 2002, 71.

Dykstra Letter to Ken Ringler.

Supplemental info:

(See prayers of Blessing ceremony, interfaith and international; see copies of the Decalogue of Assisi issued by the Vatican Feb. 24, 2002 signed by world religious leaders that rejects violence and advocates peace and religious dialogue).

(See June 19th request by the US Court of Appeals for the Second Circuit Court, Order-Docket Number 13-1668).

DOCUMENTATION

Honorary Board Members
George H. W. Bush
41st President of the
United States

Jimmy Carter
39th President of the
United States

William J. Clinton
42nd President of the
United States

Gerald R. Ford
38th President of the
United States

Honorary Trustees
Jon S. Corzine
Governor, State of New Jersey

George E. Pataki
Governor, State of New York

Michael R. Bloomberg
Mayor, City of New York

Rudolph W. Giuliani
Former Mayor,
City of New York

Board Members
John C. Whitehead*
Chairman

Dr. Josef Ackermann
Paula Grant Berry
Sir John Bond
Debra Burlingame
Russell L. Carson*
Kenneth L. Chenault
Robert De Niro
Lemuel A. DiPalma, Jr.*
Christine A. Flynt
Maurice R. Greenberg
Dr. Vartan Gregorian
Patricia E. Harris
William B. Harrison, Jr.
Lee A. Ielpi
Monica Iken
Robert Wood Johnson IV
Thomas S. Johnson*
Robert Kasdin
Amherds Katzenstein
Peter M. Lehrer*
Howard W. Lutnick
Julie Menin
Ira M. Millstein*
The Right Hon.
Brian Mulroney
Richard D. Parsons
Peter G. Peterson
Emily K. Rafferty
Kevin M. Rampe*
Thomas A. Renyi
David Rockefeller
Or. Judith Rodin
Thomas H. Riggs
E. John Rosenwald, Jr.*
Jerry I. Speyer*
Anne M. Tatlock
Daniel R. Tishman
Seryl Bhan Weldy
John E. Zuccotti*

Gardner Dykstra
President and
Chief Executive Officer

Executive Committee Member
Ex Laton

World Trade Center
Memorial Foundation

May 11, 2006

Mr. Ken Ringler, Jr.
Executive Director
The Port Authority of NY & NJ
225 Park Avenue South, 15th Floor
New York, NY 10003

Dear Ken:

Pursuant to our recent meeting, I am writing to confirm our mutual understanding about the cross-shaped artifact at Ground Zero.

We believe wholeheartedly that this important and essential artifact belongs at the World Trade Center site as it comprises a key component of the re-telling of the story of 9/11, in particular the role of faith in the events of the day and, particularly, during the recovery efforts. Its presentation will help to convey, with sensitivity and significance, this critical part of the story to the many visitors expected to come to the site for years to come.

We have further explored the issue with members of the Lower Manhattan Clergy Council and New York Disaster Interfaith Services, who fully endorse our understanding that as a public institution, the World Trade Center Memorial Foundation should present this artifact in a way that tells the story of 9/11 and not as an object of veneration. As a public institution, we will not explicitly offer religious services in association with the artifact. Here again, the Clergy Council was fully and emphatically in agreement.

We look forward to working with the Port Authority and others who care about the artifact to ensure the temporary and secure placement of it during construction on the site, and to its meaningful return to the site – where it belongs – for its eventual long-term installation, most likely at the World Trade Center Memorial Museum.

Sincerely,

Gretchen Dykstra

proof of going into 9/11 Museum

One Liberty Plaza, 20th Floor, New York, New York 10006
T 212 312 8800 F 212 312 7931
www.buildthememorial.org

TOTAL P.01

Sent: Thu, Aug 18, 2011
Subject: Apology to Father Brian Jordan, O.F.M. and Holy Name of Jesus Parish of NYC

Dear Father Jordan,

After I accepted a job as a paralegal in a law firm in the humble town of Green River, Wyoming, <u>three</u> days into working there, the attorney which I worked under,   accepted an assignment to draft and file a Complaint on behalf of American Atheists. I was out of a job since I relocated to Wyoming (following my husband's relocation) for a year, and was so happy to gain employment in a law firm (an arena where I worked for over 18 years).

Anyway, as her paralegal, I became apart of an action which I felt was wrong from the get-go, but nonetheless followed instructions and orders to research, edit, etc., matters connected to the Atheists' Complaint. I was appalled you and your parish were included as defendants on the Complaint; completely uncomfortable with associating with the Atheists group; and felt that the Atheists were "way out there" in whining about the placement of the WTC cross in the memorial - especially since it brought comfort to many and has 9/11 history.

Slightly over three weeks into working there, I resigned my new position. Admittedly, my departure was mostly based on the very heavy, dark and negative environment there, but my guilt of participating in that lawsuit brought about much angst and was, in part, why I needed to get away from that place.

Please accept my apology to you and Holy Name of Jesus Parish. May Christ be with you. I hoping for forgiveness, I am,

Very truly yours,

[Names omitted for privacy.]

UNITED STATES COURT OF APPEALS
FOR THE
SECOND CIRCUIT

At a stated term of the United States Court of Appeals for the Second Circuit, held at the Thurgood Marshall United States Courthouse, 40 Foley Square, in the City of New York, on the 19th day of June, two thousand fourteen,

Present:

Reena Raggi,
Gerard E. Lynch,
Denny Chin,
        Circuit Judges.

American Atheists, Inc. Dennis Horvitz,
Kenneth Bronstein, Jane Everhart,

Plaintiffs-Appellants,

Mark Panzarino,

Plaintiff,

v.

Port Authority of New York and New Jersey,
World Trade Center Memorial Foundation/
National September 11 Memorial and Museam,

Defendants-Appellees,

State of New Jersey, Governor Chris Christie,
Silverstein Properties, Inc., Lower Manhattan
Development Corporation, Church of the Holy
Name of Jesus, Brian Jordan, World Trade Center
Properties, LLC,

Defendants.

ORDER
Docket No. 13-1668

Amicus curiae The Becket Fund having challenged plaintiffs' standing in this case, the parties are directed to file on or before July 14, 2014, supplemental briefs of no more than 15 double-spaced pages on the issue of standing.

Plaintiffs' brief should, at a minimum, clarify both the injuries alleged and legal theories relied on to support standing.

Further, to the extent plaintiffs allege that they have been "injured in consequence of having[] a religious tradition that is not their own imposed upon them through the power of the state," First Am. Compl. ¶ 5, because individual plaintiffs view use of the challenged "cross, a Christian symbol, to represent all victims of the 9/11 Attacks" as "offensive," "repugnant," and "insult[ing]" to them as atheists, see id. ¶¶ 6-7, plaintiffs should explain how such offense states a cognizable constitutional injury in light of Town of Greece v. Galloway, 134 S. Ct. 1811, 1815, 1826 (2014) (stating that "[o]ffense . . . does not equate to coercion" merely because government body exposes persons to prayer "they would rather not hear and in which they need not participate"); see also id. at 1826 (citing approvingly to Elk Grove Unified Sch. Dist. v. Newdow, 542 U.S. 1, 44 (2004) (O'Connor, J., concurring) ("[T]he Constitution does not guarantee citizens a right entirely to avoid ideas with which they disagree."); cf. Cooper v. U.S. Postal Serv., 577 F.3d 479, 489-91 (2d Cir. 2009) (recognizing standing where plaintiff was offended by direct contact with religious displays at postal facility nearest his home and was advised to alter his behavior); Sullivan v. Syracuse Hous. Auth., 962 F.2d 1101, 1106-10 (2d Cir. 1992) (recognizing standing where plaintiff was offended by religious after-school program in community center of public housing development in which he lived).

To the extent plaintiffs allege that the challenged cross display "marginalizes them as American citizens," First Am. Compl. ¶ 6, they should explain how this states a particular and concrete injury to them rather than an abstract stigmatization of atheists generally. See United States v. Hays, 515 U.S. 737, 745-46 (1995); Mehdi v. U.S. Postal Serv., 988 F. Supp. 721, 731 (S.D.N.Y. 1997) (Sotomayor, J.).

To the extent plaintiffs reference the Memorial and Museum's receipt of government funding and their own status as taxpayers, see First Am. Compl. ¶¶ 4-5, 32-33, to invoke standing under Flast v. Cohen, 392 U.S. 83 (1968), they should clarify (a) the source of the alleged funding, i.e., federal, state, or local; and (b) whether funds were transmitted pursuant to taxing and spending authority. Plaintiffs should then explain how they satisfy the "logical link" and "nexus" requirements of Flast, see Arizona Christian Sch. Tuition Org. v. Winn, 131 S. Ct. 1436, 1445 (2011), particularly if the funds were "unrestricted," First Am. Compl. ¶¶ 32-33.

Catherine O'Hagan Wolfe
Clerk of Court

Decalogue of Assisi for Peace

On January 24, 2002, religious leaders from around the world gathered in Assisi, Italy. They included Pope John Paul II and a number of Catholic cardinals; Bartholomew I, spiritual leader of all Orthodox Christians; a dozen Jewish rabbis, including some from Israel; 30 Muslim imams from Iran, Iraq, Saudi Arabia, Egypt, and Pakistan; dozens of ministers representing Baptists, Lutherans, Anglicans, Methodists, Presbyterians, Pentecostals, Disciples of Christ, Mennonites, Quakers, Moravians, The Salvation Army and the World Council of Churches; and dozens of monks, gurus and others representing Hindus, Buddhists, Sikhs and Zoroastrians and native African religions. Their meeting culminated in a commitment to peace adopted by all present. It is called the "Decalogue of Assisi for Peace."

1. We commit ourselves to proclaiming our firm conviction that violence and terrorism are incompatible with the authentic spirit of religion, and, as we condemn every recourse to violence and war in the name of God or of religion, we commit ourselves to doing everything possible to eliminate the root causes of terrorism.

2. We commit ourselves to educating people to mutual respect and esteem, in order to help bring about a peaceful and fraternal coexistence between people of different ethnic groups, cultures and religions.

3. We commit ourselves to fostering the culture of dialogue, so that there will be an increase of understanding and mutual trust between individuals and among peoples, for these are the premise of authentic peace.

4. We commit ourselves to defending the right of everyone to live a decent life in accordance with their own cultural identity, and to form freely a family of his own.

5. We commit ourselves to frank and patient dialogue, refusing to consider our differences as an insurmountable barrier, but recognizing instead that to encounter the diversity of others can become an opportunity for greater reciprocal understanding.

6. We commit ourselves to forgiving one another for past and present errors and prejudices, and to supporting one another in a common effort both to overcome selfishness and arrogance, hatred and violence, and to learn from the past that peace without justice is no true peace.

7. We commit ourselves to taking the side of the poor and the helpless, to speaking out for those who have no voice and to working effectively to change these situations, out of the conviction that no one can be happy alone.

8. We commit ourselves to taking up the cry of those who refuse to be resigned to violence and evil, and we are desire to make every effort possible to offer the men and women of our time real hope for justice and peace.

9. We commit ourselves to encouraging all efforts to promote friendship between peoples, for we are convinced that, in the absence of solidarity and understanding between peoples, technological progress exposes the world to a growing risk of destruction and death.

10. We commit ourselves to urging leaders of nations to make every effort to create and consolidate, on the national and international levels, a world of solidarity and peace based on justice.

Included in the July 23, interfaith cere.

The Most Reverend Timothy M. Dolan, STD, DD
Archbishop of New York
Archdiocese of New York
1011 First Avenue
New York, New York

PERSONAL
AND
CONFIDENTIAL

August 16, 2010

Your Excellency,

   Greetings. I am respectfully requesting a face to face discussion or some quality phone time concerning the Cross at Ground Zero presently located at St. Peter's Church on the corner of Church and Barclay Sts. A controversy is simmering and I would like to resolve this matter quietly rather than engage in a public debate!

BACKGROUND The Cross at Ground Zero was discovered by a union construction worker on Sept. 13, 2001. I presided over a formal blessing ceremony on Oct. 4, 2001. The Cross was relocated on Ground Zero property at the corner of Church and Cortland Sts. On Feb. 14, 2002. After a hotly contested debate, a compromise was reached in which the Cross was transferred to St. Peter's Church on Oct. 5, 2006. It was verbally agreed and a letter was presented by the WTC Memorial Museum to invite the Cross to be part of the Memorial Museum upon its completion. The WTC Memorial Museum has requested the transfer of the Cross to the Museum come mid October of this year. What has occurred is a reconsideration by Father Brian Jordan, the Executive Board of the union-based Building and Construction Trades Council led by Gary LaBarbera; Edward Malloy of the New York State Building Trades and many union construction workers who had served at Ground Zero. Why the reconsideration? Because the Cross looks like a Cross in its present site at St. Peter's Church. After examining the visuals for the location of the Cross in the proposed site it does not look like a Cross but a mere artifact! It does not need to be said that this Cross has given sacred comfort through the years! It is more than an artifact, it is a sign of God's presence!

PRESENT STATUS We have had two meetings with the WTC Memorial Museum, the last being Aug.9 in which Fr. Kevin Madigan participated. Gary LaBarbera, Edward Malloy, Richard Shierer and I all presented the views of the building trades, the Cross does not look like a Cross in the proposed Memorial Museum. The building trades prefers to leave it at St. Peter's Church. Fr. Madigan said he made a promise to a benefactor when Cardinal Egan was Archbishop. That would mean, The Cross at Ground Zero will have to go in the near future. None of us want a battle with Fr. Madigan but we do want increased prominence of the Cross IF it is to go to the Memorial Museum. I do have some constructive ideas to resolve this matter behind the scenes. This is the reason I request a conference with you .

Sincerely,

Father Brian Jordan, OFM

Thos Most Reverend Timothy M. Dolan, STD
Archbishop of New York
Archdiocese of New York
1011 First Avenue
New York, New York   Sept. 16, 2010

Your Excellency,

    Greetings. Last month on Aug. 16, I sent a fax to you concerning the Cross at
Ground Zero which is presently located at St. Peter's Church on the corner of
Church and Barclay Streets. Your secretary informed me that he placed it in your
desk for review. I am not sure if you have seen it as of yet. Nevertheless, since
Aug.16 much activity has occurred. The rank and file of the union construction
workers plus their own Executive Board and Council of Delegates have strongly
asserted that they very much prefer to keep the Cross at St. Peter's rather than
going underground to the World Trade Center Memorial Museum where they
believe will be lost among many other artifacts.

    Edward J. Malloy of the NYS Building and Trades Council and Gary LaBarbera
of the NYC Building and Trades Council and I have met with the management of
the Memorial Museum and voiced our concerns that the Cross should presented as
a Christian Cross within a prominent place. We have yet to receive a satisfactory
response. We hear excuses and that a museum is not a church. They do not want
to favor one religion over another. My response is that over 2100 of the 2800
victims killed on 9/11 were either Roman Catholic or Christian. The Cross was
discovered by a union construction worker and many people to this very day find
great comfort in the Cross. After a careful period of reflection, I fully concur that
the Cross should remain at St. Peter's Church and should continue to serve as a
Christian Cross above the ground and outside rather than be lost among artifacts
underground and inside.

    Gary La Barbera informed me that he raised this point with you after the Labor
Day Mass on Sept.11, 2010 in front of other labor leaders. He received the distinct
impression that you also favor keeping the Cross at St. Peter's. If that is true, I am
so gratified and relieved. We should keep the living sign of our faith for all of the
People of God to see and not hide our lamp of faith under bushel baskets!

            Sincerely,

            Father Brian Jordan, OFM

13-1668-cv
American Atheists, Inc. v. Port Authority of N.Y. & N.J.

UNITED STATES COURT OF APPEALS

FOR THE SECOND CIRCUIT

August Term, 2013

(Argued: March 6, 2014   Decided: July 28, 2014)

Docket No. 13-1668-cv

AMERICAN ATHEISTS, INC., DENNIS HORVITZ, KENNETH BRONSTEIN, JANE EVERHART,

Plaintiffs-Appellants,

MARK PANZARINO,

Plaintiff,

— v. —

PORT AUTHORITY OF NEW YORK AND NEW JERSEY, NATIONAL SEPTEMBER 11 MEMORIAL AND MUSEUM AT THE WORLD TRADE CENTER FOUNDATION, INC.,

Defendants-Appellees,

III.   Conclusion

To summarize, we conclude as follows:

1.   Displaying The Cross at Ground Zero in the National September 11 Museum does not violate the Establishment Clause because:

a.   the stated purpose of displaying The Cross at Ground Zero to tell the story of how some people used faith to cope with the tragedy is genuine, and an objective observer would understand the purpose of the display to be secular;

b.   an objective observer would not view the display as endorsing religion generally, or Christianity specifically, because it is part of an exhibit entitled "Finding Meaning at Ground Zero"; the exhibit includes various nonreligious as well as religious artifacts that people at Ground Zero used for solace; and the textual displays accompanying the cross communicate its historical significance within this larger context; and

c.   there is no evidence that the static display of this genuine historic artifact excessively entangles the government with religion.

2.   In the absence of any Establishment Clause violation or any evidence of discriminatory animus toward atheists, the Museum did not deny

41

T·H·E· TABLET

You Can Also Read
Us on the Web at
www.thetablet.org

Lenten Meditation on Ground Zero Cross

▲ by Father Brian Jordan, O.F.M.

After conducting the 10 a.m. Ash Wednesday service in the chapel of St. Francis College, Brooklyn Heights, I asked those attending to please pray for me since I would be attending a federal appeals court hearing the next day in Foley Square.

I was the Franciscan priest who blessed the Ground Zero Cross on Oct. 4, 2001. In July , 2011, a host of institutions, elected officials and I were sued by an atheist organization for supporting that the Ground Zero Cross be inserted into the National September 11 Memorial & Museum. Although I have since been removed from the frivolous lawsuit, the atheists continued their action against the National September 11 Memorial & Museum.

In the first round of litigation, Judge Deborah Batts ruled in favor of the museum on Good Friday, 2013. The museum could keep the Ground Zero Cross for public display as part of the history of 9/11. Immediately afterward, the same atheist organization filed an appeal. The oral arguments were set for March 6, 2014, one day after Ash Wednesday. I noticed the symbolism between Holy Week 2013 and Lent 2014 right away.

After my Ash Wednesday service, Professor Susan Saladino, head of the Department of Nursing at St. Francis College, raced up to me and said, "You are not going there alone? I am going to get nurses from a nearby hospital, nursing students and myself to join you tomorrow. Where is this court house?" she demanded.

I was truly moved by this offer since my own pro-bono attorney, Matthew Dowd of Wiley Rein LLP, could not attend. I gave her directions and the time of the appeals hearing at the Thurgood Marshall Court House in downtown Manhattan. Although I was quite gratified by Professor Saladino's offer, I figured it would be impossible for her to gather many people in less than 24 hours.

The next morning, after an early Mass in the Gowanus section of Brooklyn, I took the subway to downtown Manhattan and walked up the

steps toward Foley Square. The first sight I saw was a row of TV cameras interviewing a few members of the small atheist organization who filed the appeal. (Again, they are a small group who do not represent the viewpoints of all atheists in America.) About 12 atheists were there.

Finally after two-and-a-half years, I was meeting face-to-face the very people who sued me on my birthday on July 25, 2011. I could have been angry but I pitied them. They looked haggard and lost. I thought, "These people are responsible for all this unnecessary pain and sorrow? God forgive them."

Then I entered the court house by myself awaiting the hearing in court room No. 1703 at 9:28 a.m. Since I never heard back from Professor Saladino, I assumed she and her students would not be present. Well, ye of little faith! Was I wrong? Exactly two minutes later, Professor Saladino and 15 students sat next to me, behind me and in front of me for this pivotal case involving the Cross at Ground Zero.

Never Felt Alone

The nurses and nursing students were young, energetic and caring. They were genuinely interested in this case. I was overwhelmed with joy and relief. Their presence, prayers and support were extremely touching. God has been with me during these 12-plus years of caring for the Cross. I have never felt alone fighting for the Cross and I certainly was not alone at this crucially important appeals hearing.

The procedure for oral arguments in federal appeal court begins with the lawyer representing the appellants, in this case, the American Atheists Association. Then the lawyer representing the National September 11 Memorial & Museum is provided equal time with his argument of why the Cross at Ground Zero should remain in the museum. Finally, the lawyer for the American Atheists Association has a three-minute rebuttal.

Although I am not a lawyer, I was surprised how unorganized the attorney for the American Atheists

Association was. He strayed from the main issues and seldom gave direct answers to the intelligent and penetrating questions by the three-judge panel. The lawyer for the museum was clear and succinct. He convincingly stated that religion was part of the historical experience of 9/11. (This was one of the same points I made in my amicus brief to the court.) The Cross is an artifact in the museum.

He then brilliantly asserted, "The Museum is neither a proponent nor opponent of religion. It is neutral."

However, he contended that the Ground Zero Cross is an artifact that was discovered on site as a direct result of 9/11. The atheists' request to insert a plaque about atheists should not be included in the museum

because it is not a historical artifact discovered at the 9/11 site.

After the oral arguments, one of the judges said that they will deliberate over these arguments and legal briefs and then issue a decision within a couple of months. While exiting for the elevators, I overheard some of the atheists' sympathizers groan aloud, "I think we are going to lose a second time."

When we left the federal court, I thanked Professor Saladino, the nurses and nursing students for their presence and support. I thanked them for healing my wounds. When Professor Saladino asked about what wounds, I told her not the physical wounds that

▶ See Page 28

▲ Franciscan Father Brian Jordan, standing with laborers and emergency workers in 2001, blesses a 17-foot-tall cross formed by steel beams that was recovered from the rubble of the World Trade Center in Manhattan. A group called American Atheists filed suit in federal court to have the cross removed from a permanent exhibit to be displayed in the National September 11 Memorial & Museum.

may not have been lost in vain.

Comfort and console us, strengthen
us in hope,
and give us the wisdom and courage
to work tirelessly for a world
where true peace and love reign
among nations and in the hearts of all.

* * *

Speech

I feel many different emotions standing
here at ground zero, where thousands
of lives were taken in a senseless act
of destruction. Here grief is palpable.
The water we see flowing toward that
empty pit reminds us of all those lives
that fell prey to those who think that
destruction, tearing down, is the only
way to settle conflicts. It is the silent cry
of those who were victims of a mindset
that knows only violence, hatred and
revenge. A mindset that can only cause
pain, suffering, destruction and tears.

*"This place of death became
a place of life too, a place of
saved lives, a hymn to the triumph of life over the prophets of destruction and death,
to goodness over evil, to reconciliation and unity over
hatred and division."*

The flowing water is also a symbol
of our tears. Tears at so much devastation and ruin, past and present. This is
a place where we shed tears, we weep
out of a sense of helplessness in the face
of injustice, murder and the failure to
settle conflicts through dialogue. Here
we mourn the wrongful and senseless
loss of innocent lives because of the
inability to find solutions that respect
the common good. This flowing water
reminds us of yesterday's tears but also
of all the tears still being shed today.

A few moments ago I met some of
the families of the fallen first responders. Meeting them made me see once
again how acts of destruction are never
impersonal, abstract or merely material. They always have a face, a concrete
story, names. In those family members
we see the face of pain, a pain that still
touches us and cries out to heaven.

At the same time, those family members showed me the other face of this
attack, the other face of their grief:
the power of love and remembrance.
A remembrance that does not leave us
empty and withdrawn. The name of so
many loved ones are written around the
towers' footprints. We can see them, we
can touch them and we can never forget
them.

Here, amid pain and grief, we also
have a palpable sense of the heroic
goodness people are capable of, those
hidden reserves of strength from
which we can draw. In the depths of
pain and suffering you also witnessed
the heights of generosity and service.
Hands reached out, lives were given. In
a metropolis that might seem impersonal, faceless, lonely, you demon-
strated the powerful solidarity born of
mutual support, love and self-sacrifice.
No one thought about race, nationality,
neighborhoods, religion or politics. It
was all about solidarity, meeting immediate needs, brotherhood. It was about
being brothers and sisters. New York
City firemen walked into the crumbling
towers with no concern for their own
well-being. Many succumbed: their
sacrifice enabled great numbers to be
saved.

This place of death became a place
of life too, a place of saved lives, a hymn
to the triumph of life over the prophets
of destruction and death, to goodness
over evil, to reconciliation and unity
over hatred and division.

In this place of sorrow and remembrance I am filled with hope as I have
the opportunity to join with leaders
representing the many religious traditions that enrich the life of this great
city. I trust that our presence together
will be a powerful sign of our shared
desire to be a force for reconciliation,
peace and justice in this community
and throughout the world.

For all our differences and disagreements, we can experience a world of
peace. In opposing every attempt to
create a rigid uniformity, we can and
must build unity on the basis of our
diversity of languages, cultures and religions, and lift our voices against everything that would stand in the way of
such unity. Together we are called to
say no to every attempt to impose uniformity and yes to a diversity accepted
and reconciled.

This can only happen if we uproot
from our hearts all feelings of hatred,
vengeance and resentment. We know
that that is only possible as a gift from
heaven. Here, in this place of remembrance, I would ask everyone together,
each in his or her own way, to spend a
moment in silence and prayer. Let us
implore from on high the gift of commitment to the cause of peace. Peace
in our homes, our families, our schools
and our communities. Peace in all those
places where war never seems to end.
Peace for those faces which have known
nothing but pain. Peace throughout this
world God has given us as the home of
all and a home for all. Simply PEACE.
Let us pray in silence.

(Moment of silence.)

In this way the lives of our dear ones
will not be lives that will one day be
forgotten. Instead, they will be present whenever we strive to be prophets
not of tearing down but of building up,
prophets of reconciliation, prophets of
peace. ■

U.S. Visit: Visit to
School in Harlem

Pope Francis

*Pope Francis encouraged an audience
of New York Catholic school students
and immigrants to live with joy and
dare to dream. He also highlighted the
immigrant experience — in a way children could understand, comparing it to
seeking acceptance and making friends
in school, not always an easy place for
them to fit in or find their way. "They
tell me that one of the nice things about
this school ... is that some students come
from other places and many from other
countries." Pope Francis told students
and a group of immigrants at the Our
Lady Queen of Angels School in Harlem,
where he visited Sept. 25. "I know that
it is not easy to have to move and find a
new home, to meet new neighbors and
new friends," the pope said. "At the beginning it can be pretty hard. ... Often you
have to learn a new language, adjust to a
new culture. ... There is so much to learn!
And not just homework." The message
continued the pope's call for inclusive*

Law Journal

TUESDAY, JULY 29, 2014   Serving the Bench and Bar Since 1888   An **ALM** Publication

©2014 ALM MEDIA PROPERTIES, LLC

Circuit Upholds 9/11 Display Of Cross-Shaped Metal Beam

BY JOHN CAHER

A CROSS-SHAPED beam found in the wreckage of the 9/11 terrorist attacks can be displayed at the Ground Zero museum without violating the Establishment Clause because the artifact helps tell the story of the attacks without endorsing religion in any way, a unanimous panel of the U.S. Court of Appeals for the Second Circuit ruled on Monday.

The judges rejected a challenge by American Atheists, an organization which objected to displaying the relic and then demanded public recognition that nonbelievers were among victims and rescue workers.

In a 3-0 opinion by Circuit Judge Reena Raggi, the judges parsed the U.S. Supreme Court's precedent on church-state overlap—*Lemon v. Kurtzman*, 403 U.S. 602 (1971)—and found no constitutional reason to either bar the item from public display or to order a commemoration to atheists.

American Atheists v. Port Authority of New York and New Jersey, 13-1668-cv, arose from the Southern District, where Judge Deborah Batts granted the defendants summary judgment last year (NYLJ, April 3, 2013).

But it is rooted in the discovery of the beam on Sept. 13, 2001, while hundreds of workers and volunteers were rummaging through

A cross-shaped beam recovered from the wreckage of the World Trade Center on display in 2005. It is now an exhibit in the 9/11 museum.

the debris in search of survivors and remains. One construction worker, Frank Silecchia, found a 17-foot column and cross-beam that resembled a Latin cross. The item was erected at the recovery site and became a symbol of hope and healing. It was blessed by a Franciscan priest, who began offering masses at the site for Ground Zero workers.

Over the years, the cross was preserved and stored at various locations until it was permanently moved to the September 11 Memorial and Museum site. The site includes an outside memorial, and an indoor museum beneath the memorial.

At issue in *American Atheists* was whether a government-supported museum could display a symbol with obvious religious significance without overstepping the Establishment Clause.

The Second Circuit's analysis relied primarily on *Lemon v. Kurtzman*, and the three-part test the Supreme Court established to guide the lower courts.

Under the so-called *Lemon* test, a government action is neutral and constitutionally accept- » *Page 2*

Online

✈ The Second Circuit decision is posted at nylj.com.

U.S. Agrees to Sentence Reduction in Carjacking Case

BY ANDREW KESHNER

A FEDERAL judge who has questioned whether a nearly 58-year sentence was overly harsh for

remedy injustices," Gleeson wrote.

Holloway, 57, is scheduled to be re-sentenced by Gleeson on Tuesday after once

criminalizes the use of a firearm during a crime of violence and carries stiff penalties. Specifically, the statute metes out mandatory sentences that run consecutive to the sentence for the criminal act.

TRANSFER AND BLESSING CEREMONY OF THE WORLD TRADE CENTER
CROSS, JULY 23, 2011 AT 9:30 AM TO ITS FINAL HOME—THE WTC MUSEUM

A. THE BLESSING CEREMONY WITH HOLY WATER AND PRAYER

1. FIRST BLESSING "GIVE PRAISE TO OUR CREATOR, GOD THE FATHER,
   WHO CREATED HEAVEN AND EARTH. GOD THE FATHER IS THE FATHER
   OF ABRAHAM WHO IS FULLY EMBRACED BY JUDAISM, CHRISTIANITY
   AND ISALM. WE ARE SISTERS AND BROTHERS OF THE SAME GOD
   THROUGH SHALOM, SALAAM AND PEACE. BLESS ALL THEIR
   RESPECTIVE MEMBERS WHO DIED HERE ON SEPT. 11, 2001"

2. SECOND BLESSING "GIVE PRAISE TO OUR REDEEMER, GOD THE SON,
   WHO WAS FULLY HUMAN AND FULLY DIVINE. JESUS CHRIST DIED FOR
   OUR SINS AND ROSE FROM DEATH FOR OUR SALVATION. THE
   OVERWHELMING NUMBER OF THOSE WHO DIED ON 9/11 WERE
   CHRISTIAN, ESPECIALLY ROMAN CATHOLIC. BLESS THE LOCAL
   CHURCHES WHO GAVE WITNESS THAT FATEFUL DAY—ST. NICHOLAS
   ORTHODOX CHURCH THAT WAS DESTROYED AND SOMEDAY TO BE
   REBUILT; ST. PAUL'S CHURCH THAT PROVIDED OUTSTANDING
   HOSPITALITY FOR MANY; AND ST. PETER'S CHURCH THAT SERVED AS
   A TEMPORARY MORGUE AND THEN HOST FOR OUR CROSS FOR THE
   PAST FIVE YEARS. BLESS OUR CHRISTIAN ECUMENICAL MISSION."

3. THIRD BLESSING "GIVE PRAISE TO OUR SANCTIFIER, GOD THE HOLY
   SPIRIT WHO HAS SUSTAINED US IN PATIENCE AND PRAYER. 50 DAYS
   FROM TODAY, WE WILL HUMBLY RECALL THE TENTH ANNIVERSARY
   OF SEPT. 11, 2001. IN THE SPIRIT OF PENTECOST WITH THE VARIOUS
   LANGUAGES AROUND THE GLOBE, LET US REMEMBER ALL THE
   NATIONS THAT LOST LOVED ONES ON 9/11. ALTHOUGH, THEY MAY
   HAVE WORSHIPPED BUDDHISM, HINDUSIM, SHINTOISM AND OTHER
   FAITH TRADITIONS FROM THEIR FARAWAY HOMELANDS; THEY ARE
   CLOSE IN OUR HEARTS NOW AS ALL ARE WHO DIED ON THAT DAY AND
   LEFT MANY LOVED ONES. WE ALL SHARED GRIEF—MAY WE ALL
   COMFORT ONE ANOTHER AS SISTERS AND BROTHERS THROUGHOUT
   THE WORLD!" BLESS OUR GLOBAL INTERFAITH MISSION!"

4. FOURTH BLESSING " AS THE PEOPLE OF GOD, WE WILL TRY TO LIVE
   IN PEACE AND HARMONY AS PROMISED IN THE DECALOGUE OF ASSISI"

September 25, 2015- The day Pope Francis visited the 9/11 museum.